# AGAINST
## THE NATION

ROBERT OGMAN

# AGAINST THE NATION

## ANTI-NATIONAL POLITICS IN GERMANY

new-compass.net

*Against the Nation:*
*Anti-National Politics in Germany*
2013 © by Robert Ogman

ISBN 978-82-93064-20-6
ISBN 978-82-93064-21-3 (ebook)

Published by New Compass Press
Grenmarsvegen 12
N–3912 Porsgrunn
Norway

Design and layout by Eirik Eiglad


New Compass presents ideas on participatory democracy, social ecology,
and movement building—for a free, secular, and ecological society.

New Compass is Camilla Svendsen Skriung, Sveinung Legard,
Eirik Eiglad, Peter Munsterman, Kristian Widqvist,
Lisa Roth, Camilla Hansen, Jakob Zethelius.

new-compass.net
2013

# CONTENTS

**Acknowledgements:** This book would not have been possible without the encouragement from and dialogue with Martina, Olaf, Spencer, and Peter, amongst others. Thank you also to New Compass for helping me turn the manuscript into a book, and for the opportunity to present this topic to a wider audience. The research was conducted with the support of a scholarship from the Rosa Luxemburg Foundation.

— Robert Ogman

**1**

# INTRODUCTION

I n March 2009, just months after the outbreak of the global economic crisis, 50,000 people marched through the streets of Berlin and Frankfurt declaring, "We won't pay for your crisis!" It was part of an international day of protest against the negative material impact endured by the general population for the crisis and neoliberal crisis management.

The broad coalition that included labor unions, alter-globalization associations, the Left Party, student organizations, anti-capitalist, anti-fascist and radical Left groups, brought together widely divergent perspectives regarding the root and potential solution to the crisis. In Frankfurt, this was strongly shown on the question of nationalism.

As the Left Party leader Oskar Lafontaine began his speech at the closing rally, he only managed to get a few words out before being pelted with eggs by demonstrators who drowned him out, chanting, "Never again Germany!" and "Refugees Stay, Deport Lafontaine!"

The 2,000-person Social Revolutionary and Anti-National Bloc who claimed responsibility for the disruption, described Lafontaine's appearance as a "provocation" because of his past support for nationalist positions. As former head of the Social Democratic Party, he signed policies deeply curtailing asylum rights, and supported the construction of detention centers in North Africa to prevent refugees from reaching Germany. He also blamed migrants for wage-suppression and cuts in social expenditures,[1] and supported restrictions on their access to the social welfare system.[2]

Whereas the Bloc targeted Lafontaine for his policies and positions, these were not seen as mere personal failures, but rather as the result of systematic pressures. Instead of facing and confronting these structural conflicts and contradictions of capitalism, they argued, Lafontaine sought to "solve" them within the framework of nation-states.[3]

In the end, this approach "comes to its logical conclusion": that "in this society, social provisions belong only to [national] citizens alone"—to those of this nation-state—"and the rest of the world must be kept out with force." The criticized Lafontaine wrote in his own words: "[in a] modern nation, the responsibilities of the state must be guaranteed, above all to care for those who are its citizens, and for those who contribute to the finances of the community."[4] According to this logic, the state is obligated to "protect its citizens [and] prevent parents from becoming unemployed, because of foreign workers who take their jobs for low pay."[5]

Nationalism has been a long-standing historical challenge for the Left. Yet, while critiques of nationalism have been articulated by various Left figures throughout the 20th century, the emergence of an explicitly anti-national tendency and social movement discourse only first emerged in the political conjuncture that began with the fall of the Berlin Wall in 1989. Previously, the dominant Left orientation relied on a positive affirmation of the "nation." The Old Left's call for proletarian *inter*nationalism sought to build solidarity between different national working-classes, while the New Left's anti-imperialism meant supporting "national self-determination" in the Global South.

With the opening of the Berlin Wall and the subsequent "German reunification," a strong resurgence of nationalism was felt in both East and West German states. It came not only in the guise of neo-fascism, which erupted across Europe, but in a popular nationalist euphoria across the political spectrum. It was not limited to the German province, but advanced in the mainstream press, as well as in policy decisions strengthening the national border and the ethnic character of the state, and justifying Germany's geopolitical goals on the international level.

An anti-national critique was born in the struggles of social movements against this nationalist wave. Not only did these movements reject national*ism*—understood as national chauvinism or national antagonism—but also nationalism's foundation, "the nation" and the nation-state as such.[6] This represented a clear break with the Left's inherited positions on nationalism.

The anti-national tendency that emerged in the post-1989 setting had a negative orientation towards the nation. For them, the nation-state was the engine of nationalism, not the means for overcoming it. In no shape or form could "the nation" be the social force that would or could overthrow capitalism. Nor could it herald in an emancipatory social order or even exist in a post-capitalist society. The abolition of capitalism could not coincide with the nation.

In response to the nationalist resurgence of the early 1990s, anti-fascist and anti-racist perspectives took on an increased importance for the Left. Yet each had their limitations. While anti-fascism became a pole of identification for many social movement participants in the early 1990s, and Anti-Fascist Action groups sprung up out of the ground to combat the burgeoning neo-Nazi movement, anti-fascism was circumscribed by a narrow focus on the fascist movement and ideology. Confronting the broader and more complex nationalist resurgence required new analytical tools and forms of political intervention.

Anti-racism was also a central perspective for the protest movements of this period, and linked to a variety of projects, including direct support for refugees and victims of racist violence, and countering the re-nationalization of collective identity during and immediately following the "unification" process. Yet this perspective could not address the power ambitions of the expanded Germany in the new geopolitical situation, closely connected to the logic of international capitalist competition between states. The "colonization of Eastern Europe," as the movement described the German state's international political ambitions, was not based on racial ideologies.

It was in this context that a specifically anti-national perspective therefore emerged to address a wide variety of social and political developments. It incorporated both anti-fascism and anti-racism, yet transcended both of them with the aim of grasping a broader and more fundamental political dynamic centered around the German nation-state in the post-socialist period.

The anti-national Left was therefore not the product of abstract theoretical reflections. Rather, it emerged out of the concrete struggles against resurgent nationalism in the country during "German reunification."[7] Those involved in this small radical Left tendency insisted that the new social and political terrain required the formulation of new political questions. The result of this practical and theoretical engagement was not an amended leftist worldview, in which the inherited tenets would be supplemented with an opposition to the nation. Instead, the encounter with nationalism resulted in a fundamental reorientation of a broad set of political assumptions, and produced a deep restructuring in the content and contours of Left politics and practice.

As a result, the established Left position on nationalism, which viewed it as nothing more than a form of propaganda used by manipulative elites to gain popular support, was contradicted by the clear production of nationalism from below, through the push for "unification" amongst the general population, and the swelling in popular racism. The view that nationalism is merely the distortion of an otherwise positive collective expression, which the Left should simply re-direct towards the "correct targets," was revealed as a dangerous delusion in the face of extreme violence against asylum seekers and immigrants in the early 1990s, and the popular support for harsh restrictions on migration. As a result, the anti-national debates broke the bounds of a neatly defined concept of nationalism, and began to interrogate the topic of the nation and nation-state more intensely.

The critique of nationalism, the nation, and nation-state has important relevance for movements beyond Germany. In fact, it was in light of the U.S. Left's failure to counter nationalism and antisemitism within the movement and society more broadly, that sparked my original interest in the German anti-national tendency. Therefore, this book begins with a look at the U.S. context during the last decade, focusing specifically on the anti-globalization, anti-war/anti-imperialist, and Occupy movements there. I also outline some attempts from within these movements to go beyond such trappings.

Afterwards, I set the background for the anti-national movement in Germany, closely explaining the nationalist resurgence and the social, political and economic events following the opening of the Berlin Wall in November 1989. I cover the social, political and economic changes during these years, especially the "reunification" of East and West Germany, the spike of racist violence from the German civilian population against migrants and asylum seekers, the accompanying media campaign against them, the sharpening of the ethnic character of citizenship and immigration laws, the abdication of asylum rights, and the geopolitical strivings of West Germany in the international context.

The origins of the anti-national tendency are then described through two campaigns initiated in the early 1990s. The first was the mobilization against "German reunification" in 1989/1990, under the slogan "Never Again Germany!" (*Nie Wieder Deutschland!*). It was directed against the geopolitics of the German state, and its power ambitions on the European and global stages, following the collapse of the East-West Block confrontation. Yet, the movement was also strongly opposed to the adaptation and conformity of the public and of sections of the Left to these trends, and therefore had a strong focus on the bottom-up elements of the events of 1989/1990.

While this mobilization gave birth to the anti-national tendency, the latter did not develop in a linear fashion, but rather its critique was taken up, renewed and reformulated by diverse social movement actors of the radical Left political and cultural scene of West Germany, in their responses to divergent forms and dimensions of the new nationalism in the years following. As a wave of popular racism and nationalism swept across the country in the early 1990s, a concerted effort under the slogan "Something better than the Nation" (*Etwas Besseres als die Nation*) was organized, aimed at halting the physical violence of the German public against migrants, and at developing a counter-power to nationalism amongst the public, in the media, and in state policies. Rather than targeting the geopolitical agenda of the state, this group focused on the domestic scene, confronting racist and populist nationalism, and public policy undermining migrant rights.

In these two campaigns, you get a deep look at the movements' origins and some of its core principles. They are however only two examples of the ongoing development of an anti-national political tendency and critique which has developed over the last two decades. The movement has moved into various areas, for example: criticizing historical revisionist narratives that posits Germany as a victim of World War Two; opposing a critique of "globalization" that presents capitalism as a foreign, Anglo-American phenomenon that is destroying otherwise healthy "national communities," cultures or nation-states; and, critiquing support within the Left and the broader society for radical Islamic movements following the attacks of September 11, 2001, the second *Intifada*, and the U.S. invasion of Iraq in 2003. Anti-nationalists are also active today, for example, in the current protests against the economic crisis, where they oppose Leftists who blame migrants for unemployment or wage dumping.

These examples are not meant to provide a comprehensive list of the development of the anti-national Left over the last two decades, but rather point to some highly divergent attempts to confront different expressions of nationalism in Germany in this period.

The core aspect of the anti-national critique, is that it does not seek to "solve" the problem of nationalism through pluralism. It does not advance concepts such as multiculturalism, a multiethnic Germany, or a pan-European or post-national identity. It does not try to expand the category of the nation to be more inclusive. Instead it seeks to overthrow it completely or to break it open. The project does not flee into an *abstract* universalism, but directly counters the concrete forms of nationalism existent in their social context. It does not affirm pluralism as a political strategy, but harnesses the "power of negativity" to overthrow the concrete social forms of capitalist society and nation-states.

This sketch of the broad contours of the anti-national tendency will become more filled out in the specific presentations of the two mobilizations as well as in the summary of the anti-national Left tendency following the descriptions of the two campaigns. I will show how this movement, in response to concrete social and political transformations, developed a new perspective on nationalism.

In the conclusion I address the contours of the anti-nationalist perspective, contrasting it with the orientation of the traditional Left and its positive relationship with the nation, and suggest the international relevance of an anti-national critique for Leftists in other social and political contexts. I hope that my reconstruction of the anti-national struggles will reveal the theoretical framework of the anti-national critique that has developed in sections of the contemporary German Left over the last two decades. I will show how this movement, in response to concrete social and political transformations, developed a new perspective on nationalism. My aim is to increase attention on the Left in othmokjier national contexts, to the role of "the national" in contemporary social and political developments and in capitalist society more generally, in order to make it an object of critique for an emancipatory movement. And I hope to do this without giving the impression that the specific perspective that has developed in the German context represents the "correct" position, theoretical framework, or praxis. Instead, these examples represent a particular attempt to respond to new circumstances by developing new theory. Where they challenged Left dogmas, they were at their strongest; yet where they established new ones, they failed to hold onto their original critical intentions.

# 2

# THE LEFT
# AND THE NATION

The origins of this book do not lie in abstract or historical debates about the Left and the "nation," nor in an historical interest in the German Left per se. Rather it emerges out of the failure of the contemporary Left elsewhere, in the U.S., to confront nationalism and antisemitism in the movement and in society more generally. This is a longer history, and so the focus of this section will be limited to the contemporary period, from the anti-globalization movement onwards.

## Anti-Globalization Movement

The U.S. anti-globalization movement that emerged out of the successful disruption of the World Trade Organization summit in Seattle, Washington in December 1999, was traversed by both nationalism and antisemitism. This was sometimes the result of the explicit right-wing attempts to present an alternative to "globalization" through raw American nationalism. One example of this was Pat Buchanan who posited U.S. protectionism against the competition of global capitalism. Buchanan's stance even found support from some on the Left, including former Green Party Presidential candidate Ralph Nader, who referred to his relationship with Buchanan as a "cooperation of convictions."[8]

Nationalism in the anti-globalization movement was however not limited to the activities of the Right and their left-wing allies. People who would view themselves as opponents of nationalism often expressed such ideas unintentionally. It was the result of a particular kind of understanding of "globalization," viewing it as destroying "culture," oppressing "the nation," and usurping national sovereignty. As a bulwark to this process, the nation-state was held up as the counter-power. In some instances, a binary was imagined between a supposedly harmonious, productive, national community and a hierarchical, parasitic, global, abstract force. As a result, "globalization"— and organizations like the World Trade Organization, the World Bank, the International Monetary Fund, and the World Economic Forum—were understood as capitalism, while countries as such were thought of as victims.[9] That is, rather than targeting capitalist society, it was the institutions of capitalist coordination on the inter-state level that were targeted, for supposedly disturbing an otherwise well-functioning order. This often left the relations of production underlying the capitalist system wholly untouched, in fact, sometimes even heroized as a counter to "globalization."

## Anti-War and Anti-Imperialist Movements

Following the attacks of September 11, 2001 and the resulting "War on Terror," an anti-globalization framework was supplanted by an anti-war and vulgar anti-imperialist one. The binary worldview between nation/globalization was intensified in a particular way. Now a perceived conflict between nations/nation-states on the one side, and international financial institutions/"globalization" on the other became a binary of a similar kind, where "oppressed nations" were dominated by imperialist states, the latter being represented as the United States and Israel.[10]

This led to accommodations with political Islamist movements and regimes: Naomi Klein and Arundhati Roy praised reactionary groups of the Iraqi "insurgency";[11] "anti-war" protesters claimed "We are all Hezbollah!"; Left intellectual Judith Butler praised Hamas and Hezbollah as "progressive" and "Left";[12] and "peace" and "social justice" activists met with Iran's President Mahmoud Ahmadinejad.[13]

Nationalism and antisemitism on the U.S. Left is also the result of direct attempts of some leftists to court American nationalists and right-wing libertarians as allies. Just like Nader, Alexander Cockburn, the editor of the left-wing newsletter and website *Counterpunch*, saw a potential ally in Buchanan, the isolationist Right, and the right-wing libertarian Ron Paul.[14] Cockburn sought partners in assorted right-wing and nationalist individuals, and his newsletter carried a text by Alison Weir, President of "The Council for the National Interest," promoting a modernized form of the blood libel.[15] And it ran an article by Michael Neumann urging the Left to trivialize antisemitism. In it,

Neumann wrote: "Some of this [antisemitic] hatred is racist, some isn't, but who cares? Why should we pay any attention to this issue at all?"[16]

Aside from particularly conscious efforts to work with the Right, other U.S. leftists rely on websites of the Right, for example, *Antiwar.com*, as their source of information and opinion. The website was extremely popular during the height of the Iraq War. It is run by the "anti-interventionist" libertarian Right, and is part of the right-wing populist tradition.[17]

Nationalist perspectives also are present in the U.S. Left in the adoption of the "Israel Lobby" conspiracy,[18] which presents U.S. foreign policy as being dictated by Israel and its American "agents." This was seen in the positive reception of the book *The Israel Lobby and U.S. Foreign Policy*,[19] written by conservative, neorealists John Mearsheimer and Stephen Walt.

Left critics such as Noam Chomsky, criticized the thesis of these authors as "not very convincing." Instead of "the Lobby," he argued, the determinants of U.S. foreign policy was the "strategic-economic interests of concentrations of domestic power in the tight state-*corporate* linkage."[20] But Chomsky's and similar positions were often marginalized in a milieu dominated by common references to the power of the "Zionist lobby."

Underlining the Israel Lobby argument is the assumption that U.S. foreign policy in the Middle East has been a failure. But Chomsky points out that this is only the case if you misunderstand who the policy is supposed to serve. For neorealists such as Mearsheimer and Walt, there is a conflation of "national interests" and the material interests of the U.S. population. For Chomsky, it is quite clear that U.S. foreign policy has not been a failure for the interests it represents, which is that of capital, with particular focus on the arms and energy industries, but also a broader geopolitical strategy in the region to ensure those interests.

Rather than advancing a counter-hegemonic project, the real appeal of the "Lobby" thesis is that it "leav[es] the US government untouched on its high pinnacle of nobility, [...] merely in the grip of an all-powerful force that it cannot escape," explains Chomsky.[21] The positive Left reception of Mearsheimer and Walt has led to the adoption of a nationalist perspective—in which the interests of U.S. capital and those of the U.S. population are assumed to be the same—and an antisemitic one—in that those interests are said to be usurped by Israeli interests. In its worst forms, it has fostered a context where right-wing terms such as "dual loyalists"[22] and "Israel firsters" have entered the left, and a left-McCarthyist streak can be felt whereby "leftists question the loyalties of American Jews."[23]

While many leftists who adopt the Lobby thesis may distance themselves from the more explicit expressions of antisemitism and U.S. nationalism, the structure of Mearsheimer and Walt's neorealism relies on an argument of the foreign corruption of an otherwise healthy "national interest." Mearsheimer and Walt's particular alternative to U.S. "global dominance" is a more flexible one in which the most important regions of U.S. strategic importance would be kept in balance by playing potential hegemons against one another, in order to keep them out of the regions where the

U.S. dominates. Where this strategy fails, U.S. troops should be sent in to put down the potential competitor, and then leave again once it is pushed back.[24]

Bill Weinberg also critiques *The Israel Lobby and U.S. Foreign Policy* as reversing the relationship between the U.S. and Israel, and of advancing an "American nationalist right position with overtones of xenophobia and (however much the charge has been abused) anti-Semitism."[25] Not only does Mearsheimer and Walt's text inverse this relationship, it uncritically accepts "American interests," treating them not as the result of U.S. capital, but of a foreign group which controls the state from behind the scenes. This nationalization of political analysis is often accepted in sections of the U.S. Left.

### The "Occupy" Movement

If the attacks of September 11, 2001 changed the political context for the Left, the outbreak of the global economic crisis in 2007/08 realigned the political terrain once again. In the early 2000s, the momentum of the anti-globalization movement was stopped short by the rapid change in political mood as the "war on terror" came to frame societal debate. In response, a vulgar anti-imperialist position came to the fore. In its worst variant, leftists supported the binary worldview of global power struggles advanced by the Bush administration, in some cases, simply inversing it by lending tacit support to some of the most reactionary forces abroad, so long as they could be construed as "anti-imperialist."

Since 2007/08, the economic crisis has realigned the political context, with wide-ranging implications for left political opposition. The Obama presidency, the retreat from U.S. foreign military deployment in Iraq, the great recession, and the Arab Spring have all contributed to this. The result has been the re-emergence of the question of social class. A new social movement has been born under the label "*Occupy Wall Street.*"

Yet, the *Occupy* movement has not been free from nationalist (and antisemitic) trappings. These closely resemble those of the anti-globalization movement, in which a purported national community supposedly was being threatened by outside forces. A similar position is found at times in the *Occupy* movement, with the defense of a "real, honest, productive" economy or community against "financial, parasitic" finance. The latter, represented as the "1%," is said to not belong to the unitary body of the former.

With this conceptual framework, multiple incidents of antisemitism occurred, especially in the unwieldy, first days and weeks of the protests, both at the encampments and on the web. In New York, one sign urged passerby and protesters alike to investigate the supposed Jewish character or "Zionist control" of Wall Street.[26] Participants on the web-forum of Occupywallst.org repeatedly pushed this theme, suggesting that critics should have their (apparently religious) backgrounds checked, and that those criticizing antisemitism were conducting a "witch-hunt." Additionally, a video of a participant of the *Occupy* protests in Los Angeles caught her charging that "Zionist Jews are running the big banks and the Federal Reserve."[27]

While New York City and other *Occupy* groups have made explicit statements condemning discrimination and racism, the attraction of antisemites to the protests needs to be explained. While the movement today is clearly understood as a class-oriented movement focusing on drastic wealth disparity in the country, its political origins were rather more ambiguous. Despite its somewhat leftist reputation, the magazine *Adbusters,* responsible for originally drafting the call to occupy Wall Street, has a problematic political history, delving at one point into antisemitism with an article calling out the Jewish faith of leading neoconservative figures.[28]

The magazine's original call to protest had a vagueness about it which left it open to nationalist interpretations. It did this by advancing a "beyond Left and Right" position, and therefore assuming a collective unity beyond political perspectives. For example, the statement claimed to represent something that "all Americans, Right and Left […] can stand behind."[29] And the only unifying thing they could come up with is an opposition to "corruption." Their attempt to go beyond politics resulted in their positive view of the Tea Party. The conservative movement, or its political values or platform, should not be opposed, but rather *transcended*. We should "[take] a step beyond the Tea Party movement," *Adbusters* urged.

Yet, precisely which elements ought to be left behind? The call did not criticize the Tea Party's race-baiting, the scapegoating of the poor and working-classes, the free market ideology, the support for austerity measures, or the nationalist framework. Instead, the magazine advised *Occupy* to learn from the Tea Party by avoiding the "helpless [entrapment] by the current power structure." Are the real limitations of the Tea Party its vulnerability to outside forces—its "domination" from think tanks and commercial television broadcasters—and its participation in the electoral system?

With this kind of call to action, it was little surprise then that right-wing activists were initially attracted to the *Occupy* movement. The group US Day of Rage circulated a call picking up on and sharpening the nationalist rhetoric found in *Adbuster*'s original statement. Here they too spoke of going "beyond Left and Right," yet this time, the Tea Party (as well as "conservatives") were explicitly included and welcomed to join the movement. For US Day of Rage, it was a conflict between "the nation" and "the elite."[30] They wanted to reclaim "American institutions" from their usurpation by "oligarchs" and "cleptocrats," to "take the country back," to restore America as a "great nation."

These kinds of statements opened up the movement even further to the political Right. Activists from the "libertarian Right" around Ron Paul and the neo-fascist cult around Lyndon LaRouche participated in the early days of the protest. Today they continue to praise the movement on the Internet. Additional praise came from white nationalist groups as well.[31]

One participant of the New York City protest on September 17, 2011 described the gathering as so politically mixed that "[i]t was not immediately clear if [it] was a movement of the Left or the Right, or what it wanted."[32] There was, he continues, a "sizable contingent" of people "holding signs for a variety of right wing, economic libertarian, and 9/11 conspiracy themes." Yet, as he explains, the movement began to solidify its leftist orientation: "By the end of the first week the movement's public image had become more traditionally left, primarily focused on economic inequality and reinvigorating democracy."

The positive references in *Adbuster*'s call to the anti-globalization movement, the Arab Spring and the Spanish *Indignados*, affirmed anarchists, socialists, direct actionists, community organizers, and labor movement activists in their efforts to organize a class-based response to the crisis, around the slogan "We are the 99%!"[33] Yet this slogan, like much of the movement's political content has a certain ambiguity about it that leaves it open to different interpretations. Whereas the slogan on the one hand turns the growing disparity of wealth into a tool for political mobilization around economic class, it also resonates with nationalist, conservative and right-wing thought, when this 1% is treated as foreign to the unitary body of the 99%, seen in their eyes as "the nation."

While the vague political content of the movement has left it open to this kind of interpretation, it is quite clear now that the movement is one of the Left, centered on economic justice. It cooperates with unions and workers protesting layoffs, with community organizations resisting municipal budget cuts and school closures, with homeless activists in defending social services under threat, with heavily-indebted home-owners threatened with foreclosures, with low-wage workers against exploitation.

The movement also shows efforts to go beyond a national framework, particularly in its cooperation with immigrant groups. *Occupy* played a critical role, for example, in bringing together the immigrant rights movement with the official labor movement in the Mayday demonstration in New York City. Groups across the country have supported immigrants threatened with house-foreclosure and job layoffs and cooperated with immigrant tenant activists in protesting intolerable living conditions. If a subtle national framework does in some sense exist in the movement, it may be understood as a radically open form of collective identity.

The antisemitic statements that appeared on web forums and at the margins of the protests were largely over-shadowed by the nearly 1,000 people who danced in the streets to celebrate the Jewish New Year in New York City in September 2011. In other cities, the holiday of *Sukkot* was also celebrated at the *Occupy* encampments, the construction of the traditional makeshift shelter built in defiance of regulations against tents and other structures.

Like the examples given of the anti-globalization and anti-war movements, the instances of nationalism in the *Occupy* movement do not define it as a whole. Instead, I present them to warn against these tendencies, which are themselves latent in the movement, rather than mere aberrations of it. The examples here point to limitations and problems, when participants adopt a national framework. Attempts on the Left to counter such positions and to develop critiques of nationalism and antisemitism also deserve mention, and that is what I turn to now.

## Countering Nationalism on the Left

In response to right-wing involvement and ideas in the anti-globalization movement, Anti-Fascist Forum published a short collection of articles, *My Enemy's Enemy: Essays on*

*Globalization, Fascism and the Struggle against Capitalism.*[34] The book not only scandalized right-wing involvement in the movement and right-left collaboration, but also raised deeper questions regarding the *content* of anti-globalization critiques. As with the book *Confronting Fascism: Discussion Documents for a Militant Movement*, the book highlighted the tradition of right-wing or reactionary "anti-capitalism."[35]

A significant amount of the book was dedicated to a Dutch anti-racist and anti-nationalist group, *De Fabel van Illegaal* ("The Myth of Illegality"). It tells how the group, after having initiated the anti-globalization campaign against the MAI (Multilateral Agreement on Investments) in 1997 in the Netherlands, eventually withdrew from the campaign due to the high level of right-wing participation.[36] Not unlike the anti-national Left in Germany, this experience resulted in the raising of new political questions about leftist radical work and the content of an emancipatory critique, and it had deep implications for the group's political practice. *De Fabel* felt the need to find alternatives to an anti-globalization framework, and to "develop explicitly left-wing analyses and campaigns connected to international solidarity."[37]

After concluding that attempts to "integrate anti-capitalist, anti-patriarchal, and anti-racist analyses in[to] the campaigns against free trade" were unsuccessful,[38] they came to view right-wing participation in the anti-globalization movement as "not a coincidence"—it was rather "*caused by structural flaws in the campaigns*."[39] They explain: "the problem lies in the focus of the campaigns: free trade. Ideologically separating and criticizing international or foreign capital simply does not fit into left-wing politics."[40]

This meant that efforts to include statements against nationalism within campaigns targeting "globalization" or "free trade" had no effect, because "their central concept, the supposed 'globalisation,' forces upon their readers a right-wing and nationalist conceptual framework and way of thinking."[41] According to *De Fabel*, "you can't truly analyze the reality of the capitalist system when using [the] concept of 'free-trade.'" It is flawed because it "suggests a conflict between the state and capital which does not exist in reality."[42] As a result, "the anti-MAI activists with their resistance against the 'globalization of the economy' run the risk of ending up calling for a strong state."[43] As an alternative conceptual lens, *De Fabel* offers "the concept of the international division of labor" as being "more appropriate to analyze the international shipment of capital and goods."[44]

Furthermore, the group warned that the anti-MAI campaign was "potentially antisemitic." The dominant analytical framework used in the campaign assumes a conflict between good, local, productive communities on the one side, and the transitory, international, "parasitic," speculative, financial capital on the other. They argue that this closely approximates the Right's views, and goes against the traditional Left's understanding of a conflict between capital and labor. They argue that "production and trade are inseparable parts of capitalism. And both parts of capital grow by stealing from the laborers (both paid and unpaid) and by plundering nature."[45]

Political activism always has to be considered not only in regard to its direct political effect, but also in terms of its "meta-political" implications. *De Fabel* writes, "The alliances that progressives enter into will inevitably influence the outcome of their opposition, [...] for whom we chose to walk with ultimately plays a large part in determining where we end up walking."[46] For these reasons, *De Fabel* did not view their withdrawal from the anti-MAI campaign as leaving behind a potential area of Left mobilization, but rather an effort to discover or carve out new, emancipatory pathways.

Another attempt to counter left-right overlap is the U.S. anti-fascist group "Three Way Fight" (3WF). Their name comes from the basic insight that the Left lacks a monopoly on opposition to capitalism (or at least towards its symbols), and as a result, it is not challenged by one single opponent (the Left), but also by fascist and radical Islamist forces. This became clear not only through 3WF's close observation of "anti-capitalist" positions within the U.S. white nationalist and far-right movements, but also, through the analysis of the ideology of al-Qaeda and similar movements following the attacks of September 11, 2001.

Like De Fabel and the German anti-nationalists, the 3WF acknowledges that a critique of capitalism is not the prerogative of the Left, but rather, is a perspective that takes many forms and stretches across the political spectrum. Yet in contrast to these groups, this observation has had only minor implications for the political analysis of the 3WF. For this U.S. anti-fascist group, it meant intervening against attempts by right-wing groups to participate in and influence left-wing movements or issues, most recently seen in connection with the *Occupy* movement.[47]

The 3WF's recognition of "right-wing anti-capitalism" enables them to identify one-dimensional attacks on capitalism aimed at the financial sector as belonging to a right-wing tradition. However, their focus on the right-wing *actors* behind reactionary ideas often overshadows a critique of the *content* of the reactionary ideas themselves, aside from stating that there *are* connections between these ideas and right-wing movements, in the form of anti-Jewish scapegoating, for example.

But the reactionary opposition to capitalism is not the simple result of consciously right-wing forces. Nor can its presence in left-wing movements be understood as a result of penetration and conscious infiltration of them. Exclusion of right-wing actors does not prevent *leftists* from expressing reactionary ideas, albeit in altered forms. In some cases, left-right connections are completely absent when reactionary ideas are present in left-wing movements. Instead of intentional infiltration, they emerge unintentionally, out of a binary, personalized, or reductionist critique of capitalism.

3WF's recognition that right-wing forces also present a counter-hegemonic threat, led the group to criticize the binary worldview of "us" versus "them," which they defined as one between "capitalists" and "us" (that is to say, the political Left). They replaced this bipolar worldview however, with an only slightly modified *tri*polar one, in which a "three way fight" exists between "them, them and us." In this schema, "the two sets of 'them' [...] represent the capitalists and the fascists" whereas the "us" is understood as "the anti-authoritarian revolutionary Left."[48]

While this may appear to be a framework for conceptualizing principled opposition to counter-hegemonic right-wing movements, it enabled the same kind of Left-Right alliances that the framework was designed to prevent. This was shown in the groups' open support for Hezbollah in its military conflict with Israel in 2006. The 3WF described Hezbollah as a "right-wing political movement" whose "guiding ideology is Khomeini-style Islamic fundamentalism" and whose "political ideal [is] the Islamic Republic of Iran."[49] According to them, the radical Islamist group "enforces medieval religious law, imposes brutal strictures on women and LGBT people, persecutes religious and ethnic minorities, and has executed tens of thousands of leftists and other political dissenters."[50] They continue: "This is not exactly a liberatory model."

Nonetheless, while leftists should "recognize the differences" between "leftist and rightist versions of insurgent politics" and be "warn[ed] against dangerous alliances," Matthew Lyons wrote, this was only sometimes the case. While a warning against right-wing movements and ideas in the anti-globalization is "exactly what was needed," he stated, at other times, Left-Right alliances should be pursued. He writes, "Sometimes what we need to do is defend rightist forces, in specific ways and specific situations, against a greater political threat. My enemy's enemy is not necessarily my friend, but sometimes we need to defend people who are not our friends."[51] This was the case, they argued during the war between Israel and Hezbollah in 2006 in which the group threw its support behind the "Party of God."

But why? How could an anti-fascist group critical of reactionary anti-capitalist ideology come to support a "right-wing political movement" such as this one? Simple: First, by treating this movement's enemy as the pure expression of its own opposition: Instead of a national conflict, the war between Israel and Hezbollah was treated as an anti-capitalist one; for 3WF, "Zionism" is nothing more than an "example of global capitalism."[52] And second, by avoiding to define Hezbollah as "fascist," support for whom would outright contradict the group's anti-fascist self-understanding. To achieve this maneuver, Hezbollah's antisemitism would be relativized through a direct comparison with the Nazis: Lyons writes for example, it's "quite possible that Hezbollah sometimes engages in anti-Jewish scapegoating, but the organization is not continuing Hitler's work and does not exist in order to kill Jews." Case closed. Despite their clear right-wing character, they deserve support, Matthews argues.

Therefore, despite the attempt to find a new orientation in the face of the complexities and differing directionalities of ideological and material struggles, the 3WF reverts to a vulgar anti-imperialist position defined by a binary global struggle in which capitalism is concretized in the U.S. and Israel, and even the most reactionary, non-"fascist" forces lining up against them potentially deserves support.[53]

This is the background context for this book: the failure of the Left to develop an emancipatory perspective opposed to nationalism, the nation and the nation-state. Now I will return to the specific social and political context out of which the German anti-national Left emerges.

**3**

# GERMAN NATIONALISM
# AFTER REUNIFICATION

The anti-national Left emerged in the distinct political juncture of 1989/1990, through its confrontations with a nationalist resurgence following the opening of the Berlin Wall. In this context, nationalism came to strongly influence state and international politics, civil society, and the emerging forms of collective identity. To understand the anti-national positions at this time, it is therefore important to look at these societal shifts in the early 1990s.

### Germany's New International Role

The collapse of the Berlin Wall is often cited as a pivotal event in the unraveling of the post-war era. With the collapse of the East-West order, a political conjuncture emerged concerning the future of the European order. West German Chancellor Helmut Kohl's efforts to unite East and West Germany came to play a central role in the new configuration of the European political geography. In this juncture, Germany became a major power in European and international affairs.

The economic and political benefits of the unification of West Germany (The Federal Republic of Germany, FRG) and East Germany (The German Democratic Republic, GDR) grossly outweighed the state's budgetary costs of this fusion. With the incorporation of the Eastern territories of the former GDR, the Federal Republic acquired "a much wider market and greatly expanded opportunities to evade the labour market rigidities that have depressed German economic performance in a new division of labour where low-value processes are outsourced by German firms."[54] The political benefits included "pushing the border of Western Europe further eastwards and creating a zone of stability on Germany's Eastern flank."[55]

These economic advantages pushed the world's third-largest economy to become "*the* leading power within the European Union."[56] Furthermore, the FRG moved away from advancing general European interests, "and became much readier to advance an explicit national interest" in the realm of international politics.[57]

This territorial expansion of the FRG, and its corresponding growth in international political and economic influence was met with trepidation amongst some of the leading political powers, not to mention its bordering countries. United Kingdom's Prime Minister Margaret Thatcher and the French President François Mitterrand feared that a more powerful Germany might seek to retake territories lost in World War Two, or that it might be too economically competitive in

Eastern Europe following the collapse of the iron curtain.[58] Additionally, the disappearance of the Soviet Union would mean the loss of a bulwark against these possibilities.[59]

The return to full sovereignty—following four decades of close US and Soviet Union supervision—was followed by Germany's development into an independent global power.

## National and Post-National Politics and Identity

The *political unification*—that is, the establishment of the single German nation-state out of East and West Germany—was accompanied by the reemergence of the role of "the national" in social, political and economic life domestically. It played a central role in reconstructing a collective German identity and the concomitant reformulation of historical narratives, forming a public discourse to legitimatize certain political and economic policies, and demarcating lines of social exclusion including the use of physical violence in civil society against perceived "outsiders."

The political juncture of 1989 saw collective identity in Germany transforming from what many described as a "post-national" identity into an affirmative "ethnic national" identity. The "post-national" collective identity was rooted in the international role the FRG played in the West (the *Westbindung*) and the European Union (at the time, the European Community), as well as the economic affluence of the West German population.

In the founding decades of the Federal Republic its identity was profoundly affected by its commitment to European integration. European integration acted as a very powerful force on a divided and defeated Germany seeking to re-establish its capacity to act internationally in order to lift the restrictions placed upon it after the war. It saw in European integration a policy which would give its neighbors enough confidence to lift these provisions. An export-orientated economic structure gave West Germany a fundamental interest in the creation of frameworks for opening up trade at the European level.[60]

The post-national identity amongst the population was also due to the country's post-war "economic miracle."

Economic growth helped internally to strengthen popular attachments to the Federal Republic; initially conditional on economic success, these gradually diffused into a more fundamental allegiance to the West German state. Those attachments were "post-national" and in part projected outward into "Europe." This Europeanized state identity increasingly resonated in affiliational terms at both mass and elite level.[61]

While there were positive sanctions contributing to the development of a post-national identity—including European integration and economic affluence—there were also negative restrictions preventing the public affirmation of a German national identity in the Federal Republic. These included taboos and repression, due to the shadow cast by the connection between German nationalism and racial persecution, genocide and to military conquest during the National Socialist period.

The process of denazification, Western re-education programs, and the Nuremberg and Auschwitz Trials all contributed to weakening public affirmation of a German national identity, even if such expressions did not disappear. Additionally, the revolt in the 1960s of student movements against the continuities between the Nazi-period and the post-war Federal Republic, particularly regarding government and business personnel, further prevented "the national" from playing a significant role in public discourses towards the legitimation of public policy and of collective identity.[62]

While efforts to re-establish an affirmative national identity were undertaken throughout the immediate post-war decades[63], it was the opening of the Berlin Wall that shifted the terrain, producing new conditions for an affirmative national identity.

## Reunification and National Identity

With the collapse of the post-war order and the subsequent unification of East and West Germany—a process helped by the opening of the Berlin Wall—"the nation" quickly reappeared in public discourses, which in some cases was observed by the international press with alarm. A pivotal yet often overlooked example of this process of "nationalization" is the transformation of the East German opposition movement from a left-democratic movement into one with aspirations for national unification.

The protests by students, youth, and workers, sought basic democratic rights, such as freedom of speech, press, and assembly, as well as independent trade unions and women's organizations. The main organization, *"Neues Forum,"* sought a grassroots democratic praxis for transforming the social structure from below.

The original slogan of the movement was "Wir sind *das* Volk!" ("We are *the* people!"), a democratic statement demanding the government represent and be held accountable to the people. But in Leipzig, the democratic spirit quickly mutated into a movement for national unification under the slogan "Wir sind *ein* Volk!" ("We are *one* people!").[64]

This conflict at the level of civil society between the original demand for democratic reform and the later aspirations for national unification, was paralleled in the conflict over the process of political unification. In a highly visible article published in *Die Zeit* in early 1990, German political philosopher and public intellectual Jürgen Habermas warned that the unification of East and West Germany was a delicate process in which a conflict existed with two possible outcomes.[65] According to Habermas, one should nurture and support the "republican constitutional patriotism" that had developed in the old Federal Republic by pursuing a democratic path towards unification. This was possible by means of a referendum, directly involving citizens of East and West Germany. This option was constitutionally possible by use of Article 146 of the Basic Law (*Grundgesetz*) of 1949.

Instead, the Helmut Kohl government preferred "annexation" based on Article 23 of the Basic Law, which gave the FRG the right to incorporate "other German lands" into its territory. Habermas argued that this course represented national domination over the citizens of East Germany, encouraged national chauvinism, and threatened the post-national collective identity (Habermas spoke of the "non-nationalistic self-understanding") that had developed in West Germany in the previous decades.[66]

Many feared these developments might occur at the level of both state and civil society. Author Günter Grass outright opposed reunification out of the fear that "a reunified Germany would be a colossus, laden with complexes, which would stand in the way of itself and of the unification of Europe."[67]

## German Ethnic Nation

While collective identity in the old Federal Republic was often described as post-national, its deeply ethnic character could be seen in the state's definition of German nationality, declared in the Basic Law of 1949. It stated:

> [A] German within the meaning of this Basic Law is a person who possesses German citizenship or who has been admitted to the territory of the German Reich within the boundaries of December 31, 1937 as a refugee or expellee of German ethnic origin or as the spouse or descendant of such person.[68]

This *ius sanguinis* ("right of blood") principle meant that German citizenship could only be acquired if one could prove that they are of German descent, or that they are the offspring of German citizens.[69] This definition had large implications for the patterns of inclusion and exclusion—

both during and after 1989—of millions of immigrants, based on "ethnic national" characteristics. Newcomers defined as belonging to an ethnic German community with vastly different cultural and linguistic characteristics were quickly absorbed. Their integration was well-funded by the government and they found their interests represented in the political realm. In contrast, newcomers from southern Europe who originally came to West Germany as contract workers part of the "guest worker" program and remained in the country and had families, or who brought their relatives to West Germany afterwards, were denied citizenship along with their children and grandchildren, even those born in the country.

## Citizenship, Naturalization, Immigration

In addition to this limited definition of citizenship, those seeking German citizenship were faced with a strict naturalization process, requiring a high level of assimilation. According to Simon Green, it required they "give up the majority of their cultural identity in favour of 'becoming' (not just legally) German."[70] Based on the 1977 Guidelines on Naturalization, it "explicitly requires a very high standard of cultural adaptation by an immigrant, to include the demand of 'voluntary and lasting orientation towards Germany'," a process which can also only begin after successful integration, which itself was open-ended.[71] This left the FRG with one of the lowest naturalization rates in Europe, not rising above 0,4 percent throughout the 1980s.[72] Large numbers of immigrants, often third-generation, whose only language was German, and whose only residence had ever been the FRG, lacked German citizenship. This exclusion was compounded by the fact that non-nationals lacked the possibility of acquiring dual citizenship, in contrast to many other European states. Applicants are compelled to choose between German citizenship and that of their parents or grandparents.

Another issue related to immigration, and which became the central topic of public debates following the fall of the Berlin Wall, is that of asylum. As a correction to the massive refugee problem caused by the political and "racial" persecution of Nazi Germany, the Federal Republic's Basic Law included the right to asylum. In Article 16, it was declared that "politically-persecuted people [shall] enjoy the right to asylum."[73]

Throughout the 1980s roughly 70,000 people sought to exercise this right annually, but with the opening of the Berlin Wall in 1989, this number rapidly increased. In the following year, the number of applicants more than doubled to 193,063, the year afterwards adding 60,000 more people to the total, and the year following that, jumping above 400,000 applicants.[74] This made Germany the most popular European destination for asylum seekers.

An additional component of the transformation of "the national" following the fall of the Berlin Wall was the passing of the *Ausländergesetz*. On July 9, 1990, the "Aliens Act" was passed in parliament. This law only formalized already existing practices in the state's treatment of immigrants, making "the granting and renewal of residence permits subject to the 'interests of the Federal

Republic of Germany.'"[75] But this meant codification in the boldest terms, that the rights of non-German citizens were subordinate to the national interests of the German state. This could be understood in an expansive and flexible sense, whether according to the labor requirements of the national economy, the maintenance of social peace, just as well as demographic control. It would become fundamental for the social and political conflicts in the following years.

## National Self-Consciousness and "the Other"

The public affirmation of a proud and self-conscious German nation that emerged after the opening of the Berlin Wall was accompanied by a strong attack on those deemed not to belong to that "national community." That is, almost as soon as the division separating East and West Germany came down, new boundaries were drawn.

According to public opinion polls, the number one priority that concerned the West German public following the opening of the Berlin Wall was not that of political unification, but rather that of "foreigners" (*Ausländer*) and asylum. As Karen Schönwälder explains:

> In June 1991 aliens and asylum rocketed up the scale of themes Germans regarded as important, overtaking unification and the Gulf War, to become priority number 1 for the West Germans until February 1992. It returned to that position in the following summer and autumn.[76]

A media frenzy developed, in which a discourse about the "inundation by foreigners" (*Überfremdung*) took center stage. "The notion that Germany was being flooded, that millions were about to come from the south and east and that Germany's affluence, for some even its existence as a nation, were under threat, had been hammered into the population."[77] This was combined with political campaigns by the conservative CDU and CSU party candidates that employed anti-foreigner rhetoric to garner public support.[78]

## Spike in Racial Violence

Additionally, citizen-protests emerged in numerous West German cities against shelters for asylum seekers. This wave of anti-foreigner sentiment culminated in violent attacks on immigrants and refugees as well as other minorities. The most extreme cases were the attacks by mobs of German civilians against asylum seekers and foreign contract workers in the cities of Hoyerswerda and Rostock in 1991 and 1992.[79]

In September 1991, the east German city of Hoyerswerda became the site for a week long pogrom. For four days long, hundreds of skinheads and other German civilians gathered outside the housing complex of foreign contract workers, and under the slogan "Foreigners out!" successfully drove them out of the city. At the height of these events, up to one hundred youth physically assaulted the building with "bottles, chains, clubs, baseball bats, and Molotov cocktails," threatening to raze it to the ground. The youth were urged on by the crowds of 500 people, who shouted racist slogans, cheered on the assailants, and prevented the police from intervening.[80]

On the fourth day, the police massed outside the building, and the mob moved on to the site of the asylum seekers' residence across town. Here, a crowd of up to one thousand people cheered on 50 youth who attacked the building, until local officials removed the refugees, hence allowing the racist attacks to dictate public policy.

In another east German city, Rostock, a five-day long pogrom in August 1992 was even more intense. Nearly three thousand supporters cheered on up to five hundred attackers, led by West German neo-Nazis and skinheads, the crowd allowing the assaulters to hide amongst them. Attackers stormed the residential complex, setting it on fire, and chasing over one hundred contract workers out. As a result, the government bussed the contract workers out in the middle of the night, essentially achieving their explicit goal, to get "foreigners out."[81]

These attacks were made possible due to the passive response of the police[82], the national anti-immigrant mood, and the support from local public officials.[83] At this time, public opinion polls revealed that more than a third of the population "expressed understanding for violent actions 'because of the aliens problem'."[84] This empathy for the perpetrators, rather than the victims was mirrored in the media reports.

It was not until November 1992, after the murder of three Turkish women in an arson attack in the west German city of Mölln, and when civil society groups organized candlelight memorial marches in numerous cities, that the government made public moves to suppress such violence.[85]

Racial attacks spiked out of control during and after 1991, jumping from under 400 incidents in the previous year, to 2,720.[86] A year later, that number increased by 2,000 incidents, and then climbed even further in 1993 to 5,580.[87] For the next two years that figure dropped by 1,000 incidents each year, leaving it nonetheless at more than five times higher than before the fall of the Berlin Wall.[88]

Acts specifically categorized as violent also spiked after reunification. Whereas the majority of annual figures for the 1980s were below the 100 level, the average annual figure between 1991 and 1995 was over 1,200, peaking in 1992 to 2,000 "violent anti-foreigner incidents."[89]

Right-wing antisemitic incidents followed a similar pattern. In the 1980s the average number of incidents was 289. From reunification to the mid-1990s, that number jumped to 730, reaching a high point in 1994 with 1,366 incidents.[90]

It is also significant to note that contrary to the assumption that nationalism, antisemitism, and xenophobia are problems limited to the East, roughly twice as many violent assaults from right-wing perpetrators were committed in West Germany per year than in the former Eastern states, although the latter's smaller population meant that they were occurring at twice as high a frequency per capita as in the West.

The figures show us that both the frequency and intensity of anti-foreigner and antisemitic incidents spiked in the years following German reunification, and did not return to their pre-1989 levels.

The spike in racial violence in these years coincided with the emergence of far-right, neo-Nazi, nationalist political parties and organizations. Membership in right-wing parties, extremist organizations, and skinhead groups increased by 10,000 people between 1980 and 1995, peaking in 1992 to over 40,000 members and falling to just above 30,000 in 1995.[91] In this period, the far-right *Republikaner* Party nearly tripled its size, in 1989 jumping to 25,000 members and maintaining over 20,000 for the next five years.[92]

The total right-wing incidents spiked enormously in 1991, with a jump from 1,848 the previous year to 3,884. The following year, the figure nearly doubled again to 7,684, and then in 1993 spiked above 10,500 incidents.[93] It dipped just under 8,000 incidents in the following two years, which, in contrast to the figure ten years previously, meant a *five-fold increase*. Between reunification and 2011, more than 180 people lost their lives due to right-wing violence.[94]

## Asylum Reform

Following the media campaign and the wave of violence against asylum seekers in the early 1990s, the reverberations were also felt at the level of state policy, with the curbing of asylum seekers' rights.

On December 6, 1992 the government of the conservative CDU/CSU, the social democratic SPD, and the neoliberal FDP passed Article 16a to the Basic Law, the "Asylum Compromise," which sharply restricted asylum rights. It reduced the number of asylum seekers through a variety of methods. First, many applications were automatically rejected if the individual originated from a country on the "white list," which was considered to be a "safe country," or if they passed through one of the states bordering Germany considered a "safe third country." The process of deportations was also sped-up, with the arranging of a "fast-track procedure" at the Frankfurt airport.[95] These measures drastically restricted asylum applicants, dropping the number to fewer than 100,000 in 1998.[96]

These transformations of German politics and identity are crucial to understand the Left responses to the new nationalism in Germany since 1989. The state and civil society shifts since 1989 from a post-national to an affirmative ethnic national identity is the context in which an explicitly anti-national political orientation emerges.

# NEVER AGAIN GERMANY!

**N**ie Wieder Deutschland! ("Never Again Germany!) was the name of the mobilization organized predominantly by West German social movements and left intellectuals against West German efforts to "reunify" it with East Germany. With a set of provocative public protests in Frankfurt and Berlin in 1990, the Radical Left (*Die Radikale Linke*), together with like-minded activists, expressed public opposition to the geopolitics, resurgent nationalism, and the re-instauration of "the national" in social, political and economic discourses and in the public realm in the Federal Republic of Germany after 1989.

Relying heavily on primary source material, where participants articulated their viewpoints, I will show how activists of the *Never Again Germany!*-mobilization viewed the social and political situation at the time, and how they articulated a specifically anti-national critique. The primary material is the literature published by the central actors of these social movements, as it was expressed in two books, *Die Radikale Linke: Reader zum Kongress*, which is a collection of texts used as preparation material for the participants attending the organization's congress in June 1990,[97] and *Kongress der Radikalen Linken*, documenting the speeches delivered at the conference, the motions passed by the participants for further activities, as well as a sample of press clippings about their demonstration in Frankfurt in May 1990.[98]

## The Radical Left

The campaign was initiated by participants of the newly formed network, the Radical Left, a loose collection of left intellectuals and activists, predominantly from West German social movements. It brought together individuals from across the left spectrum, including former members of the Green Party, disenchanted by its integrative impulse, feminists opposed to the Social Democrats' reduction of women's issues to employment equality, activists from the autonomous movement (*Autonomen*), as well as members of the *Kommunistischer Bund* and the German Communist Party.[99]

Against the integrative approach of the parliamentary left, the Radical Left sought to assert "the power of negation" to band together to develop a "system-oppositional" orientation, hoping to "intervene over a wide area by means of journalism, hopefully in an increasingly organized manner, and locally in concrete, practical debates."[100]

Just a month before the opening of the Berlin Wall on November 9, 1989, they outlined their political orientation in their "Basic Principles of the Radical Left" ("Grundlage der Radikalen Linke"), where they expressed opposition to the "modernization of capitalism" with help of ecologists, feminists and social democrats.[101]

According to the Radical Left, the integration of ecologists, feminists, and social democrats into the government might "deliver a few environmental technologies into the export palette" of the state, and assure a few career opportunities for women, but it would not assure anything further.[102] They argued that these minor adjustments and concessions were part of a broader modernization of capitalism in the Federal Republic. This broad cooperation was, in their view, underlined by a nationalist perspective, which hid inequalities of socio-economic class, gender, and status, both in terms of racial discrimination against Germans with an immigrant background as well as those without German citizenship, such as temporary contract workers and asylum seekers living in the country.

This consensus-based nationalism, with its focus on the modernization of capitalism, was complicated by the rapid political developments of 1989/1990—the unexpected collapse of the GDR, the advancement of West Germany's plans for reunification, the re-instauration of a national discourse across the political spectrum and the society, and the electoral success of the far-right party, the *Republikaner*. These developments made the Radical Left push "the national question" to the center of its critique, where the target of their criticism was Germany, the Federal Republic as such and "the nation," at times warning that the expanded FRG meant the construction of a "colossus," a "greater Germany," and the emergence of a "Fourth Reich."

## The Protests of Nie Wieder Deutschland!

In May 1990 the Radical Left organized a public protest in Frankfurt against German reunification. Borrowing the words of the popular German cabaret performer Marlene Dietrich, who fled her native country during the Nazi period and performed for the Western allied troops on the front during World War Two, the demonstration paraded under the banner, "Never Again Germany!" On protest banners, speeches given at the demonstrations, and on their leaflets, the protesters expressed opposition to "German nationalism," the "colonization of Eastern Europe," and the "annexation of the GDR."[103]

An estimated 20-30,000 people, from a broad spectrum of left social movements and individuals joined the demonstration, which, due partly to the outbreak of physical violence between police and demonstrators, was covered by the national and international press.[104] The broadness of the political spectrum that participated in the protests even outdid the diversity of participants of the Radical Left itself.[105]

Yet, as the unification process accelerated, the *Never Again Germany!*-campaign faced competing oppositional positions and mobilizations. A demonstration by East and West German women's organizations managed to bring twice as many people onto the streets in Berlin at the end of September 1990 as the demonstration of The Radical Left. In contrast to the Radical Left's outright rejection of the reunification, the alternative demonstration criticized the democratic deficit of the unification process, and demanded public inclusion into it.[106]

The *Never Again Germany!*-campaign, however, maintained its influence in the radical left scene. Roughly 15,000 people took part in the "days of action" for the "re-division" of Germany (*Aktionstage für den Wiederzusammenbruch*) between September and October 1990, and 1,500 participants attended their congress in Cologne.[107]

Although the campaign opposed reunification, the participants expressed awareness that this objective was unachievable. They knew that the opponents of the reunification were far too few and weak. This observation, however, did not persuade them to cooperate in reunification in the hopes of influencing the outcome. Instead, they believed it was nonetheless correct to oppose the process. From the outset, they had stated that reunification was unstoppable. "I agree," said Radical Left participant Winfried Wolf, "there is every indication that reunification [...] is coming."[108] But this realization, Wolf argued, "doesn't change anything"—"There are projects that people *must* reject outright," despite and against the position of the majority of the population, citing as additional examples the majority's support for the death-penalty and for the prohibition of abortion.[109]

The aim of the campaign was therefore to build as strong and oppositional a movement as possible, in order to limit the worst possibilities of a nationalist revival. Wolf writes, "it is about developing the resistance as broad and massive as possible," because, "the weaker it is, the more brazen those who will profit from the reunification will prevail."[110]

## Opposing the "Aliens Act"

Parallel to their absolute opposition to the German reunification was their categorical rejection of the "Aliens Act" (*Ausländergesetz*). According to them, the political unification coincided with the FRG's domestic policy, aimed at creating a homogenous national community. In a resolution at their congress in early June 1990, they wrote: "The Aliens Act is the reflection of the German reunification, in which Germans rediscover themselves as a nation, and ban everything non-German."[111] They called upon the West Berlin-based political party, the Alternative List (*Alternative Liste*), to vote against the Act and to pressure their coalition partner, the Social Democratic Party (SPD), to do the same.

In their view, the "Aliens Act" was based on a "racist conception of the existence of a special 'German *Volk*', which is to be sealed off from immigration, from so-called 'race-mixing' with people from different backgrounds."[112] In their short resolution, they focused on the employment of both state and interstate measures of the EU to physically seal off the FRG from immigration:

> Through the Aliens Act, together with the Schengen Agreement, a new wall will be built around the Federal Republic and Western Europe, which will impede and prevent especially the people from the so-called "third-world" from entering the FRG and Western Europe.[113]

It would also prevent refugees from being able to reach the FRG, where they might apply for asylum. They refer to the statements in the Aliens Act that demand allegiance to the FRG, writing that for those without German citizenship who are living in the country,

> they will be completely subordinated to the West German political, economic and cultural relations. For those who do not conform, they will be threatened with deportation, and their political activities will be restricted, and threatened with penalties.[114]

Although this was one of only three resolutions passed at their congress,[115] concrete activities against the Act appear to have been rather marginal in the campaign, and the topic is not central to their writings. This status was criticized by Hamide Scheer, who asked at the congress: "Why is there no link between the protest against reunification and resistance to the Aliens Act?"[116]

Despite the lack of protest-activities against the Act, and the minimum amount of attention given to it in their books, the content of the resolution was extremely important for the group. It revealed the participants' universalist political demands, for open borders and opposition to migration-controls and restrictive citizenship.

## The Radical Left's Critique of Nationalism

The campaign against reunification involved multiple and interrelated aspects of an anti-national critique. The critique can be understood as having two major aspects. The first involved opposition to the FRG's geopolitics during the political conjuncture of 1989/90, both within and beyond the national territory. This included the absorption of the former East Germany into the national territory of the expanded Federal Republic, as well as the state's political and economic objectives in the international arena. Here we can mention the FRG's role in the EU and NATO and its trade relations with Eastern European states following the fall of the Iron Curtain.

The second major aspect of the *Never Again Germany!*-campaign involved the critique of the nation as a narrative or ideology of a national collectivity, and its active use by a broad variety of civil society and state actors for political objectives.

A final aspect was the development of a "negative patriotism."[117] This can be understood as a critique of the material disadvantages for both those who conform and do not conform to the imagined "national collectivity," and involves support for the most disadvantaged by their lack of membership in it. This praxis can be understood as a counter to integrative pressures in the "national community."

## *A Geopolitical Critique*

The Radical Left viewed the political developments as hovering between the modernization of capitalism and the threat of a fourth Reich. The thread connecting the two was the pervasive use of a self-confident nationalist narrative. The Federal Republic of German was, in their view, aspiring to a higher level of power and international influence, and this could either take the form of a normal state in relation to its neighbor countries, or it could regress to an aggressive, militarist state reminiscent of the National Socialist regime, with wars of conquest, racial persecution and direct domination across the continent. This feeling of uncertainty and deep fear in this political conjuncture made a mark on their writings.

In a group statement in January 1990, co-written by 100 participants of The Radical Left, they write of a "German-national frenzy" not seen since the end of World War Two.[118] After the collapse of the Berlin Wall, they argue, the Federal Republic immediately set the objective of "reunification" on the political agenda.[119]

According to them, this objective meant the state's aspirations towards increased international political power and economic influence, through the EC (later EU), its participation in NATO, and its trade relations with Eastern European countries. They warned this would lead to "third-world" conditions in Eastern Europe, dominated by Western European countries.[120] They write, "the countries that have until now belonged to the Council for Mutual Economic Assistance[121] are threatened with becoming a new 'third world', of becoming the backyard of the wealthier capitalist societies of Western Europe, and especially of the FRG."[122] According to their analysis, reunification would mean that Germany would become a controlling power in Europe. They write:

By planning to grant the GDR this "Sonderweg," the FRG sees in its confederation and unification plans first and foremost the chance to strengthen its dominance in the West and all of Europe—and with it, against the East and the South. A "re"

or new-unification would make the fourth Reich the ruling
power in Europe.[123]

Additionally, they criticized the grounds on which the
reunification took place, which they, like Jürgen Habermas
and others, saw not as an authentic unification of the FRG
and GDR affirmed by the citizens of both states, but as an
*annexation* of the fledgling East Germany by the politically
and economically strong Federal Republic. This was seen as
part of a geopolitical strategy on the part of the FRG, which
sought to increase its economic and political influence on the
international arena.

In another text, participants of the Radical Left argue
that the FRG, helped by the International Monetary Fund,
managed to compel the former GDR into reunification
by pressuring a privatization of its industries—the
establishment of a market economy and the opening to
Western investment—or to risk complete bankruptcy. Under
this pressure, the FRG managed to annex new territory
on conditions of Western capitalism.[124] This pressure gave
the flailing GDR no other option but to implement these
economic austerity plans, which resulted in the fulfillment
of Konrad Adenauer's stated objective of 1949, of the "Unity
of Germany."

According to the Radical Left, reunification was, however,
only the first step towards the EU's "colonization" of Eastern
Europe. The formation of EU financial institutions for
investment and lending in markets in formerly East Block
countries, to establish a market economy and "private
enterprise," was a means through which the FRG would

like to establish Berlin as the capital of the EU bank.[125] New member states would be allowed after they transitioned to a market economy.[126] The FRG was the "front-line state of the West's campaign to conquer the markets of Eastern Europe."[127]

On the *internal territory* of the FRG, this national "frenzy" was seen as intensifying the state's mechanisms of exclusion towards those deemed not belonging to the "national community." This was seen in economic policy that privileged employees of German decent over non-nationals on the labor market, and in immigration policy and citizenship laws, as well as in policy towards Asylum seekers.

Regarding the FRG's economic policy, the Radical Left argued that it was "anti-foreigner" (*Ausländerfeindlich*) because, immigrant groups both already in, and those striving to enter the FRG, were differentiated based on "racial" classifications. Those immigrants who could prove German ancestry, were treated as "ethnic German repatriates," and received full rights of citizenship, employment, housing and otherwise, in contrast to those immigrants who could not do so. The former group of immigrants therefore occupied a privileged position in contrast to the latter group of immigrants, based on a *Völkisch* nationalist categorization, argued the Radical Left.[128] This confirmed an "openly racist discrimination against 'foreign' immigrants in favor of those 'of German origin.'"[129] This exclusion also applied to asylum seekers in the realm of housing policy, which, according to the "decision of the administrative court of [the southern German state of] Baden-Württemberg, from August 2, 1989, asylum seekers shall not be allowed to live in residential areas."[130]

The negative effect of national narratives was however not limited to those without German citizenship, or those otherwise excluded from the "national collectivity." It also disadvantaged many belonging to this "imagined community," including wage earners and women in particular, and was part of a general swing to the Right.

The lower socio-economic classes would be negatively impacted by this, because a national narrative based on the image of a "deep horizontal, comradeship" disguised the material class inequalities of the actual population, as well as gender inequality.[131] For the Radical Left, the modernization of capitalism taking place at the end of the 1980s and early 1990s did not close the gap between these different groups, but rather intensified the polarization. They wrote: "modernization means not the improvement of living standards of all, but rather the polarization downwards and upwards," and therefore there are also "modernization losers." [132]

For the campaign against reunification, they viewed "the national question" as "overlaying the social question, simply ideologically."[133] They pointed to statements by political and business leaders who stated that reunification would have to be financed by wage cuts, and the long-term passivity of the labor unions. Politically, this would be complemented with the ban on left-wing parties that were perceived as too politically close to the GDR.

Another example of the campaign's position that the nationalist resurgence would also disadvantage people included in the "national collectivity," could be seen in their comments on gender inequality. The expected spike in female unemployment following the abdication of the GDR's gender equality laws, and women's subsequent "return" to unpaid reproductive labor in the household, would be rationalized on the grounds that women's domestic labor was a necessary contribution to the "national community."

This assumption was based on the trend in the Soviet Union, where, as the Radical Left pointed out, official propaganda advocated the "return of women to the house and kitchen: Women should 'relieve' the market of paid labor power and perform the unpaid tasks of reproductive labor completely alone."[134] For the Radical Left, the subordination of gender equality to the national market was a component of the new national sentiment.

## Nationalism from Above

Nationalism was seen partially as state ideology, employed instrumentally to win the support of the population against their own material needs, for the purpose of geopolitical objectives. According to the Radical Left, the unification of East and West Germany into an enlarged German state involved the production and circulation of a national narrative in order to garner support amongst the population for that political objective. In his talk at a conference of the *Never Again Germany!*-campaign, Hermann L. Gremliza, editor of the left magazine *Konkret*, argued that the general population's support for Kohl's reunification plans and national sentiment more broadly in the 1980s was quite low, and only increased after political leaders repeatedly pushed the issue in the framework of a "national interest."[135]

Gremliza described nationalism therefore as "an ideological program," pushed by political leaders, that imagines a collective good amongst members of a society.[136] He wrote:

> Broadly speaking, nationalism in a modern industrial state, that is, beyond a tribal society, is an ideological program, which for the ruled, for the "regular person on the street" [...] does not follow from their immediate interests, and also can not be made so. Nationalism feigns a higher collectivity, a blood-community (*volksgemeinschaftliches*) interest, which in reality does not exist in a class society.[137]

According to him, nationalism is a "fiction" that does not emerge organically from the material reality of the individuals, but is produced by political actors.[138] The commonality between citizens of the FRG and the GDR was imagined, exaggerated, or imbued with meaning beyond actuality, Gremliza argued. Reunification was seen as an effort to avoid irresolvable contradictions in West German society, and therefore a distraction for the population which was set in motion towards the objective of national communion, and who might have otherwise petitioned against material inequality within the society. This national ideology had to be produced amongst the population, and was done so through the singing of the national anthem, the national education system, military service, amongst other means.

## Nationalism from Below

While nationalism was on the one hand seen as an ideology pushed by political leaders in order to garner support from the populace, it was simultaneously seen as something emanating from the populace itself. Not only from above, but also from below. Bernhard Schmid, a participant in the campaign at the time, explained in a later reflection on the protests, that the two positions, of nationalism from above and nationalism from below, co-existed.[139] As Schmid wrote,

> the aspect of capitalism, which presents itself as victor of history and whose protagonists would now expand their economic power unhindered, was not opposed. But the essence of the historical events lays not in identifying the "class interests" of the economic leaders, but rather that there was agreement amongst all the other social classes to the unification process. [The campaign against reunification] scandalized that none of the social interests in opposition to capital were articulated.[140]

Already seen in their material before the opening of the Berlin Wall and the initiation of the *Never Again Germany!*-campaign, the Radical Left expressed opposition to the integrative aspirations of some left-wing political parties, trade unions and social movements in their critique of the "red-green delirium," which through collaborative efforts with the state and business, contribute to the growth of nationalism.

I n "German Question—Which Question?" one campaign participant, Detlev zum Winkel, argues that the reunification was interpreted amongst the German public as the end of the post-war era, which resulted in a causal chain of consequences: the end of the consequences of the Second World War for the Germans, the end of the consequences of the German defeat, and the end of the defeat.[141] The author claims that this logic was already set in motion in the 1980s with the Bitburg affair and the Historians' Dispute. If this logic is correctly observed, the psychological disposition of the population leads them to "wage war with Bismarck, with Wilhelm, with Hindenburg, with Hitler against the rest of the world, instead of waging together with the rest of the world against nationalism, militarism, racism, antisemitism, and national socialism," he claims.[142]

## Nationalism and Capitalism

According to The Radical Left, nationalism was based on the social structure of modern capitalist society. For them, it emerged from the all-against-all logic of the market economy, and the international conflict between nation-states. What this meant is that the state's ideology is also based in market competition. The conservative, neoliberal and social democratic parties, "are forcing an industrial policy to defend the dominant position of the FRG on the world market,"—at that time ranked third in global GDP—"and to build further opportunities for it," the Radical Left wrote.[143] This argumentation sees a connection between the normal pursuance of "national interests" of the modern capitalist nation-state on the international terrain on the one hand, and the *ideology* of nationalism on the other.

The growth of nationalist ideology on the part of the population, expressed in its most extreme form in the far-right political parties, had its roots in the market economy, in an environment where "the competition of all against all becomes standard conduct, on the labor market and in the 'flexibilized' production."[144] In this situation, "the 'competent' people [are] to be given free reign; the weak and those who refuse to perform are to find their deserved downfall."[145] Furthermore, for those who manage to succeed, they "must defend their advantage against those below."[146]

This "standard conduct" involves a "social darwinist radicalization" when this "hierarchical social picture" is interpreted through a national narrative. "Those who fall behind in the struggle of all against all (or those who fear it)," they wrote, "can find themselves in this portrait of society."[147] They continued: "They can assure themselves, that they have experienced injustice (or that they are threatened with it), and that their position on the lower [end of the hierarchy] ought to be occupied by others: foreigners, and racial and sexual minorities."[148]

"The feeling of superiority," they wrote, "is instable."[149] At length:

It is correct on a world map, but not for the internal social structure [within a given state territory]. Whoever has something in common with his boss towards the outside, is on the inside however on the bottom. He is only a secondary victor. This is only tolerable if one has others still further below

> oneself. If the weak, to whom one doesn't belong, gains the
> upper-hand, real wages will stagnate, housing shortages will
> develop, and children will receive no apprenticeships, the fear
> rises, that one realizes where one really is in the hierarchy: on
> the bottom rather than the top.[150]

This "realization" is expressed in the ideology of neo-Nazism. The Social Darwinist radicalization, they wrote, receives its "positive affirmation in the most vulgar form in the ideology of right-wing extremism."[151] Accordingly, "the Republicans offer their fellow countrymen [*Volksgenossen*] that the correct people will be sorted to the bottom—and not themselves." But, the far Right has not organized this situation, only radicalized it.

According to this perspective, the Republicans are "pushing the nationalist rhetoric further" than the conservative Christian Democratic Union/Christian Social Union, the neoliberal Free Democratic Party and the Social Democratic Party, but are not responsible for "organizing the basic, economic essence" of it. This was the work of the centrist parties, they argued, and the social structure of modern capitalist society.[152]

In this way, the *Never Again Germany!*-campaign viewed the far Right as radicalizing the normal competition between nation-states on the global market, elevating the reality-based picture of group inequality to an ideal, in which the FRG ought to fight for the top spot, at the expense of others. This internal exclusion results from the desire to have a feeling of superiority within the hierarchical social schema.

## Negative Patriotism and Opposition to Integration

In response to nationalism, the Radical Left also advanced a form of "negative patriotism."[153] They wrote:

> [E]very asylum seeker and immigrant from every country, which has been plundered by the FRG is closer to us than the East German "brothers and sisters" who identify with the competitive society and sing along in the "great German" choir.[154]

The nationalism would be countered with humanity and "solidarity with the weak, excluded and stigmatized."[155] They argued that everyone living on the territory of the FRG should have the right to citizenship, and those with immigrant backgrounds should be given the right to dual-citizenship rights. They declared the FRG a "multinational state" composed of people originating from many countries, and a "multinational society."[156] The implications this should have on social movements was to "express and practice this multinational character" by, for example, implicating a "change of the organizational form, [making our movement] multilingual, and [changing] the political culture."[157]

This was, however, only one element of their fundamental shift against national integration. The *Never Again Germany!*-mobilization also demonstrated opposition to an integrative impulse, which it identified not only amongst the general population, but also amongst the Left parties, the unions, and other sections of the left.

The Radical Left emphasized that they sought to develop "the power of negation."[158] For them the participation of the

Left in the developments of 1989/1990 only empowered nationalist forces and the Right. With reference to the historical integration of the German left in 1914 and 1933 into the national consensus, this contradicted their aims, and revealed a certain danger, which they drastically warned against.

Rather than seeking to influence the social and political developments through cooperating with the trends, and hoping to steer it towards the left, they recognized their position as being on the margins. According to them, there was a national consensus stretching across the political spectrum, and from the highest tiers of the state, to business interests, to trade unions, environmental organizations and other non-governmental groups, down to the ground level of individual's consciences.

In contrast to the traditional Left, which emphasized the role of market forces seeking direct access to cheap labor and resources as well as new consumer markets in the new Eastern territories, the Radical Left focused on the societal consensus supporting the drive towards unification. The latter, they argued, ought to be understood as a *national consensus*, whereby, despite the material costs to the population—the massive privatization of east German industries, the dismantling of the social welfare system, and the skyrocketing unemployment—they were convinced of a "national interest."

An anti-national praxis did not mean having to remove oneself from the social-historical context, to denounce and therefore to cleanse oneself of that which one opposes, but to discover oneself within this historical context, and to work against it. To find oneself within this history also does not mean to discover new heroes who went against the grain, and through identification with them, to remove the stain of history from oneself. Rather, as Maria Baader and Gotlinde Magiriba Lwanga wrote, one ought to:

> place oneself finally, as a woman, as a leftist, as a German, as a white person, in the history, to give up the repression and the distortions, to recognize that nationalism, racism, and antisemitism are not only weapons of the rulers, but rather also have a dynamic and function which we have something to do with, […] and therefore to create the basis for a *German anti-national movement*.[159]

In response to the political unification process, and the social and political developments surrounding it, the *Never Again Germany!*-campaign articulated a particular perspective on the question of nationalism, the nation and the nation-state. Primarily, they expressed a geopolitical critique of the Helmut Kohl government and the aspirations of the FRG to pursue purely "national interests." They criticized the aspirations of the expanding and increasingly powerful FRG, particularly on the European continent, and in Eastern Europe in particular.

For them, the political unification was however not possible without the formation of a societal consensus on the nationalist ambitions of FRG. They criticized the widespread commitment to the national project amongst people from different socio-economic classes and across the political spectrum. The societal consensus meant that even people from lower socio-economic classes supported this political program, despite the negative impact this would have on them materially. Here they referred to the sweeping privatization of East German industries, the stark rise in unemployment, the abdication of labor laws of the former GDR such as that for gender equality in employment, and others.

In traditional Marxist approach, they viewed the nationalism of the population as being a misunderstanding of their actual material interests. Benedict Anderson's description of the "imaginary political community" shows how a "community" is imaginary because "regardless of the actual inequality and exploitation that may prevail in each, the nation is always conceived as a deep, horizontal comradeship."[160] This national consensus was partially pushed by political elites and the mainstream media, but also developed from below. This distinguished the *Never Again Germany!*-campaign from projects whose criticism was primarily directed towards political elites.

According to them, the "imagined community" that is the German nation does not provide justification for the fusion of the two states. Additionally, it represented a pronounced danger in consideration of the country's past efforts to expand its territory and increase its international political role.

# 5

# SOMETHING BETTER
# THAN THE NATION

While the Radical Left had brought together diverse perspectives under a common opposition to political unification and German nationalism, the heterogeneous group did not survive. However, this was only the beginning of anti-national mobilizations. Responding to the growing neo-fascist movement, as well as the rightward drift of mainstream political discourse and public policy, a new, anti-national formation arose.

In 1992, during a wave of racist violence particularly in the East, a country-wide group of individuals under the name *Wohlfahrtsausschüsse* came together under the banner "Something Better than the Nation" (*Etwas Besseres als die Nation*). Because of the racial attacks in the cities like Hoyerswerda, Rostock and Mölln, the rapid growth of neo-Nazi organizations, the public frenzy over immigration and asylum, and the passing of the "Asylum Compromise" (*Asylkompromiss*), the group decided to intervene in the public realm, at both the practical and analytical levels, to combat the "radical right-wing potential in the state and society."[161]

They did so by holding semi-public discussions on timely political issues and strategy sessions for civil society groups engaged in anti-racist work. Their major intervention, however, was a caravan of West German musicians, artists, intellectuals, and activists to East Germany, in order to support people there who were confronting the radical Right in the public space. Additionally, the *Wohlfahrtsausschüsse* coordinated a public demonstration against the passing of the Asylum Reform, by physically blockading the parliament building in Bonn in 1993.

The group's book *Etwas Besseres als die Nation: Materialien zur Abwehr des gegenrevolutionären Übels* (*Something Better than the Nation: Material Against the Counterrevolutionary Evil*), shows an attempt to develop a practical and analytical response to popular nationalism and racism, as well as to the resurgence of the far Right. They sought to address the relationship between racism and nationalism, and to show how their appearances in civil society are connected to the state level and public policy.

Like those of the *Never Again Germany!*-campaign, the participants of the *Wohlfahrtsausschüsse* were individuals on the non-parliamentary Left. They were social scientists, newspaper and radio journalists, university lecturers, artists, and political activists from multiple West German cities. They describe the campaign as having "constituted itself as an ad-hoc group of musicians, DJs, artists, authors and journalists," which had the goal of countering "the fascist attacks on migrants, gays, the handicapped, leftists and on the counterculture."[162]

As a strategy of "intervention" the group sought to develop a cultural praxis, open to people not directly involved in Left political groups, who could counter the far Right in various forms. The aim was to empower people who were opposed to the rightward drift, yet had been frightened out of the public realm. The campaign sough to support these individuals in speaking out and in contesting the reactionary political developments.

Rather than traditional political rallies, the group also sought to intervene on the cultural level, doing so by offering public concerts, aimed at supporting a counter-culture amongst the youth. Journalists and scholars intervened at the level of public debates in the press, targeting nationalism, right-wing violence, and state policies of social exclusion.

The main activities of the *Wohlfahrtsausschüsse* were organizing public meetings to discuss the new nationalism, and to strategize ways to combat it; a political and cultural tour by West German artists, intellectuals and social-movement actors through Eastern Germany, with concerts, public forums, and leafleting, to support anti-fascist initiatives there; and a mass civil disobedience protest aimed at blockading the parliamentary session on the Asylum Compromise, and therefore against the state's ability to select which people will be granted the right to stay in the FRG, and which will be compelled to leave.

## Fostering Debate and Engagement

Participants of the *Wohlfahrtsausschüsse* sought to foster public debate, critique and opposition to the new nationalism. They did so by organizing public forums as well as strategy sessions for people hoping to make their civil society engagement more successful, through theoretical reflection as well as by the development of strategies and improved coordination between initiatives.

In December 1992, individuals of the Hamburg-based group of the *Wohlfahrtsausschüsse* circulated an invitation to a meeting for an "initial discussion" about how to respond to the wave of racial violence erupting in post-unification Germany. The invitation, with the title "Our Minimum Goal" sought to bring together people to discuss the initiative under the slogan "Something Better than the Nation."[163]

In the short statement, the authors announced their aim as the "symbolic defense of the public and private space against the growing influence of neo-fascist groupings."[164] This meeting was to provide the opportunity for the "exchange of opinions about the [current political] situation, the discussion of positions and the development of perspectives for anti-racist work."[165] This would "open a forum for different approaches to such a praxis," and for the "coordination" between different groups.[166] One common project proposal was to support initiatives in the former East Germany to combat racial violence and the right-wing, where violence and harassment of immigrants and asylum seekers occurred over the course of days with no reported interruption from members of the civil society. More concretely it proposed to organize a political and cultural tour through Eastern

Germany with the holding of musical concerts and public discussions.[167]

These meetings represented some of the first public discussions held by the group, in order to analyze and organize against the rightward shift in the immediate post-reunification years. By doing so, they hoped to gain a better understanding of the shifts occurring in the post-1989 FRG, which would enable them to "intervene" in political debates taking place in the press and to counter forms of racism they experienced in civil society. With many of the participants being active in cultural fields, rather than explicitly political ones, they sought to "connect a subversive praxis in cultural as well as political spheres."[168] This would help get new people involved, those who were "outside a traditional political context."[169]

## Etwas Besseres als die Nation

In early 1993, the caravan under the title, "Something Better than the Nation," took place. It brought 250 musicians, intellectuals, and antifascist activists through the new federal states in Eastern Germany, playing concerts and holding public discussions with the intention of creating a counter-weight to the emergent far-right scene and public mood. They went specifically to cities and places where racial violence had erupted, including Rostock, Dresden and Leipzig. There they hoped to build connections with and support for people in East Germany "to challenge the Right and to confront them publicly."[170]

The tour statement from the Hamburg-based *Wohlfahrtsausschüsse* group described the feeling of deep alienation and powerlessness in observing the racial violence in Germany in early 1993, and expressed the need for both a practical and analytical response to it. They wrote:

> Germany in the Spring of 1993: The closer we look, the stranger it looks back. The only thing left for us to do then is to convert this observation into critique. You are outraged over the pogroms against "foreigners," you want to do something against it and you stand suddenly in front of a mountain of questions. You want to act *concretely* with others and you suddenly realize that you need to also be *abstract*, to develop and discuss concepts.[171]

The analysis of this nationalist resurgence, *Wohlfahrtsausschuss-Hamburg* argued, must take into account the diversity of actors behind it. Armed skinheads have their allies in the newspaper columnists. Government officials who seek to employ state measures to prevent the entry of asylum seekers into the country exist side-by-side with ordinary people who want the state to move swifter on the "Asylum question," while the Social Democratic Party's position on the issue comes increasingly closer to that of the conservatives. They wrote:

> You want to confront the baseball bat-wielding Nazi and realize he has allies in the feuilleton of your newspaper and on the book market, who formulate open or coded justifications, which will be read by many and which you have to rebuke. In the morning news you hear, that the Federal Minister of the

Interior is calling on the Western and Eastern European states for a "concerted and comprehensive defense strategy against the entry of refugees." In the bakery, a customer is enraged over the "inaction of the politicians on the Asylum question." Midday, you read in the newspaper: "On the Asylum question, the Social Democratic Party moved closer to the position of the governing coalition" and "Skinheads in the city of Halle attack the private homes of Vietnamese with Molotov cocktails."[172]

Observations like this one meant that the *Wohlfahrtsausschüsse* saw a multiple and heterogeneous set of social actors behind the nationalist resurgence. Yet, they warned against a personalization of the issue, that is, of limiting ones understanding of nationalism or racism to a problem of distinct individuals, from which society could be freed from as long as those individuals are stopped. They argued that there was a relationship between the different actors, who functioned together in an interactive way: "While the right-wing mob persecuted refugees, parliament worked feverishly on another means towards the same goal."[173] There was a "barely hidden broad coalition of Parliament, Nazi-terror, normal citizens, police and the media in a cynical interaction, which were together busy with the 'solution to the Asylum Seeker Question.'"[174]

The *Wohlfahrtsausschüsse* opposed not only the direct, brutal violence of street mobs against non-Germans, but also state measures that limited the latter's rights. The group's practical political engagement involved targeting both of these forms of nationalism.

Their objective, they stated, was not merely to demobilize the right-wing mob and to defeat direct physical violence, but also to counter the exclusion of refugees that took other forms. Here they referred to state measures such as the "Asylum Compromise." They did not seek to impact public policy, if this means that "the brutal methods of neo-Nazis would be replaced by the 'cleaner' due process of the law, [e.g.] if this means the deportation of refugees."[175] (As we will see below, they therefore directed their opposition towards the state, and sought to prevent the passing of the "Asylum Compromise.")

Yet, not only did the political Right target people with direct, physical violence and with the bureaucratic state apparatus; it also fought on the symbolic level. With "systematic terror, the far Right not only seeks the conquest and domination of the streets, public places and bars, with the use of baseball bats and firebombs, but they also seek to occupy the 'ideological space.'"[176]

For this reason, "purely praxis-oriented counter-actions that miss their mark on the content or are weakly grounded"—such as physical confrontations with neo-Nazis, which had developed in the autonomous scene (*Autonomen*) in the 1980s and continued in the 1990s, or the candlelight memorial marches—are "ineffectual" and "fatal."[177] Their object must not be limited to neo-Nazis, but to include the broad matrix of social forces that have contributed to the nationalist resurgence in the past years.

In the cities the caravan visited, they held hip-hop and punk rock concerts, aimed predominantly at youth. They also circulated flyers with their political analysis, and in Rostock they hung a plaque on the wall near the site of the attacks on the homes of contract workers and refugees in Rostock in August 1992. The plaque was a concrete effort to bring attention to the history of racial violence in the city, and to persuade the population to prevent it from reoccurring. The plaque was inscribed with a call to remember the victims of the National Socialists in Rostock, as well as those of racial violence in 1992. It included the sentence: "These experiences and the historical responsibility of the German people must be kept alive, in order to prevent violence and the contempt for mankind from repeating itself." Shortly afterwards, however, as the group documented, the plaque was anonymously removed.[178]

This was symbolic of their tour completely, which they themselves regarded as negatively or indifferently received by the population, as well as their left-wing oriented target group. It was even being opposed by leftists during their stop in Leipzig.

Andres Fanizadeh, a participant of the tour, reported that although well prepared, with enough people to defend against a neo-Nazi attack and enough journalists to prevent repressive measures by the authorities, the caravan experienced "infinite indifference" amongst the population.[179]

While they were able to carry out nearly all of their activities—including the mounting of political posters and the painting of political graffiti in public space, demonstrating through the city center with amplified political speeches—it was all ignored. And after they had left every remnant of their presence was removed:

You could graffiti slogans and hang posters on the walls against the abolition of asylum rights unhampered; simply a

> case for the building cleaners the next day. Even the sound-system and the (amplified) speeches in the city centers gained no attention from the pedestrians scurrying by. Theory discussions in the centers of Eastern subculture? The left scene had, with the exception of Leipzig, no interest in it. The concerts in the evenings: what are the musicians blabbing about? Louder, faster, harder![180]

They reported an over-whelming indifference: "It was all in vain. Between friends and enemies, you could not tell the difference."[181] Without running into neo-Nazis or being confronted by police, they left with a "crippling impression of emptiness."[182]

The aim of improving the cooperation between initiatives in East and West Germany had "completely failed."[183] The only success lay in the building of a coalition of artists, intellectuals and political groups to challenge the "repressive national-state." This success could be seen in the emergence of an anti-national critique within left-wing social movements, but also for popular audiences through newspapers as well as in music and art.

## Opposing Asylum Reform

The third significant project of the *Wohlfahrtsausschüsse* was directed against the "Asylum Compromise." The aim was to physically blockade the parliament building in Bonn through mass civil disobedience to prevent the government from passing the bill on May 26, 1993.

In the call for the blockade the *Wohlfahrtsausschüsse* criticized the strong limitations placed on asylum rights through the adoption of Article 16, Paragraph 2. The paragraph read that "asylum is not granted to those who enter from a member-state of the European Community or from a third country, in which the application of the Geneva Convention is guaranteed."[184] They argue that the Asylum Reform prevents any possibility for people to enter Germany by land.[185] In outright rejection of the state to regulate the flow of people across the national border they wrote about the Asylum Reform:

> The only way persecuted people [could reach asylum in Germany] would be to book a non-stop flight to the FRG from the prison's travel agency [in their country of origin]. The FRG has pressured mainly Eastern (European) countries to be their accomplices. They are meant to serve as an external barrier, stopping migrants and refugees heading to Germany, and therefore denying them the same freedom of movement, in whose name the GDR was taken down just some years before.[186]

This refusal to accept the state's power to control its border was stated in the following way: "The power to decide, whether someone is or is not politically persecuted of who is and who is not in an emergency situation shall not remain in the hands of political parties in parliament." Therefore, the *Wohlfahrtsausschüsse* group in Frankfurt wrote, "we oppose every selection criteria which denies residence to people who, by either want or need, choose to live in this country."[187]

Participants in the attempted blockade of the parliament building numbered between 3-4,000 people.[188] The heavy police presence managed to prevent the blockade from stopping the parliamentary session, and was only successful in inconveniencing some ministers. As three entry points to the parliament were blocked, many ministers had to arrive by boat or by helicopter. "Most ministers learned what it feels like to have ones 'land route' blocked," wrote Wolf Wetzel[189] and continued:

> The majority of the representatives [could only access the parliament building with a boat] and found this detour humiliating and dishonorable. Instead, they would have wished for a strong police operation [to uphold] their self-evident right of freedom of movement.[190]

Therefore, while the protest had the effect of disrupting the parliamentary session and bringing the issue into the press, it did not manage to prevent the passing of the "Asylum Compromise."

### A Structural Analysis

The *Wohlfahrtsausschüsse*'s analysis of nationalism included multiple elements. One of these was their understanding of nationalism as a popular and well-established aspect of society that was affirmed throughout the population, rather than a marginal phenomenon on the edge of society. They based this argument on the fact that the assailants against asylum seekers and contract workers in Rostock for example found support in the adult population, such as the crowd of onlookers who cheered and applauded the assaults, sought to prevent police intervention, made similar statements as the rioters, and defended the latter as victims of "foreign domination" ("*Überfremdung*").

In their "Against the *Völkisch* Center" ("Gegen die völkische Mitte") one of the participating groups of the *Wohlfahrtsausschüsse*, the *Autonome l.u.p.u.s-Gruppe*, expressed this view when they described a society-wide nationalism supported by diverse social actors and with various means: "whether arsonists or politicians who speak of 'being inundated by foreigners,' whether with combat boots or briefcases, whether in the office, in the administration, in the public services or on the streets."[191]

According to them, the enormous spike in right-wing crimes "did not need to be committed in spite of the police, the leading democratic politicians or the majority of the population," but rather took place under the protection of the police, public officials and the majority of the population.[192]

They further argued that it is insufficient to physically confront neo-Nazi mobilizations. Instead, a social-movement practice must be developed in accordance with the "knowledge and historical experience" that shows that "racist and *völkisch* actions originate in the center of society," and that they have "their *legal* basis in state institutions, in the democratic political parties, in the police and judicial system, in the medicinal and cultural thought structures."[193]

This argumentation was expressed in the callout by the *Wohlfahrtsausschuss-Hamburg* for the caravan "Something Better than the Nation," who stated that racism is not the result of individual racists, but instead based in the social structure of modern society:

> Racism outrages the most, when it is expressed directly from or carried out directly against people. This creates the impression, that racism can be fought by fighting racists alone. But the idea "Nazis out = Racism out" does not work. Believing that racism exists only "through" individual racists, leaves the racist structures of reproduction in modernity unconsidered.[194]

The statements reveal that their view of nationalism was not limited to single, marginal actors, but rather, they saw it as being part of the social structure.

## Interaction between State and Society

Another aspect of the *Wohlfahrtsausschüsse*'s analysis was their multi-actor view of nationalism which they saw as an interactive dynamic between the levels of state and civil society,[195] where the economy, the state, the society and the media all play critical roles.[196] In order to understand this dynamic, they argued, one "must always proceed from a structural, current historical 'unity of action', on which, multiple powers participate in, and in no way leads back to one single source."[197] Nationalism could not be understood as a mere ideological tool of manipulative elites; it had a structural existence in capitalist nation-states. Yet, nation-states do not in themselves lead towards nationalist or ethnic violence. There are important subjective factors involved. Responding to the concrete political developments of their time, they focused on the relationship between the "media frenzy" over asylum and immigration, the physical violence of the population, and the constitutional reform of the asylum law, that is, of state policy.

## International Competition

Another element of the *Wohlfahrtsausschüsse*'s analysis of nationalism, was their argument that racism and nationalism are not limited to individuals, but rather that "the individual and institutional levels support one another."[198] This is especially true for societies organized upon a market economy with a dynamic of 'cutthroat competition':

> As in every market-based society where a permanent cutthroat competition shapes every aspect of life, in Germany people are daily tested for their real or alleged "weaknesses" (based on the reigning standards), to sort them out as inferior competitors.[199]

However, the material opportunities for individuals are dependent not only upon their personal performance, but also upon other forces, particularly the national economy. Under these conditions, a structural dynamic produces hope in wage-earners that "their capitalist does good business with them and with others" so "that they can continue to be wage-earners tomorrow."[200] That is to say, the material advantages and disadvantages are based not solely on the individual, but also on the social structure that gives individuals advantages and disadvantages.

But while the nation might be imagined as a "community" for collective improvement amongst market actors, it is simultaneously a "hunting ground," they argued:

> The market subject is bound to the fate of the nation. It is towards this fate that it must relate itself, it is in its framework that it collects its fundamental experiences in the struggle

for survival and that is how it forms its identity. In conflict situations it must serve the nation, and this is also how it expects protection by the nation: The slogan "Germany for the Germans!" does not necessarily mean "Foreigners out!" but above all "Germans first!"[201]

The leverages of concrete advantage in this struggle include rights to employment, housing, and social services amongst others:

The German passport and the "Alien Act" actually determine people's life chances. In March 1993, the [Department of Labor] issued the binding guideline that persons with a German passport ought to be placed in preference.[202]

The structure of the nation-state and the power of belonging to the collectivity represented by that state, means a structural pressure to grab at the advantages offered, especially in times of crisis. They wrote:

Because being German procures a tangible competitive advantage over "foreigners" inside the national realm, it becomes more attractive in times of sluggish conjunctures to publicly identify with the "ethnos."[203]

Returning to the topic of the political unification and the homogenization of the citizenry, they wrote that the nation-state unleashes a dynamic that produces "potential racists" out of its citizens.[204] This is so as long as the citizens "advance the fiction of a unitary *People* with a common history of descent and 'identity,' and strive—despite a heterogeneous reality—toward the realization of a process of homogenization of the citizenry."[205]

Furthermore:

> In the end, it is claimed that the state border and "ethnic" lines are precisely congruent and the People is not an imaginary community of atomized individuals but a community of common descent.[206]

Because the citizen "must hope in the international assertiveness of 'his' state" and "that it retains 'global standards,'" they wrote, nationalism is also produced due to international dynamics between competing states on the global market.[207] Therefore, they claimed, "racism emerges out of the everyday life of an export-nation which participates on the world market."[208]

The formation of the *Wohlfahrtsausschüsse* out of a collection of non-parliamentary activists and public intellectuals, came as a response to the practical and theoretical urgency to respond to the nationalist resurgence and racist violence as well as the government's "Asylum Compromise." Intervening in public debates, building a counter-current to the right-wing, the group sought to affect the course of social and political events of the time.

Through this engagement they developed and circulated analyzes of the relationship of racism to nationalism, and of the dynamic interplay between forces at the level of the state and civil society. Their engagement led them beyond opposition to national*ism* and to a position that rejected the nation form as such. In contrast to approaches that see nationalism as inter-ethnic conflict, the *Wohlfahrtsausschüsse* sought to discover the motives behind those who raise "the national question" at all. For the group, nationalism emerges out of the social structure of capitalist society, and the lived reality within nation-states. It results not simply from elite strategies of manipulating populations, but also from below, from diverse actors within market societies.

Their political protests targeted concrete actors, such as neo-Nazi skinheads, and concrete policies, such as the Aliens Act, yet they strove to connect this with their theoretical orientation that nationalism was a society-wide phenomenon, and did so through their writing.

**5**

# ANTI-NATIONAL
# PERSPECTIVES

The campaigns *Never Again Germany!* and *Something Better than the Nation* were amongst the first explicitly anti-national projects that emerged in Germany and set the grounds for an anti-national tendency that continues to this day. But what precisely set these projects apart from the left's inherited stance on the nation? What are the contours of the anti-national position today? And what relevance might an anti-national perspective have for anti-capitalist struggles elsewhere?

### The German Left on Nationalism Before 1989

With the absolute rejection of the nation, the Radical Left, the *Wohlfahrtsausschüsse,* and the countless anti-national projects that followed them, proposed an explicit break with the left's inherited positions on "the national question." For both the Old and the New Lefts, the relationship to the nation was one of affirmation (that is, of "self-determination"), and of peaceful cooperation with other national collectivities.

"Proletarian internationalism" framed the problem in terms of the relationship between national groups, and not in regards to the production and reproduction of these groups themselves and their structural existence in capitalist nation-states. The Communist Manifesto's rallying cry—"Workers of the World Unite!"—targeted the antagonisms between workers of different countries (in the form of national hostilities), but not nations as such.

The German New Left had strong reservations towards any positive associations with Germany. "The distancing from one's own nation," writes Andrea Ludwig, "[was] constitutive for the emergence of the student movement during the 1960s."[209] She elaborates:

> The fact that the majority of Germans at least tolerated the Nazi crimes and were hardly inclined to hold [Nazi criminals] accountable after 1945, and to initiate a process of self-criticism, was an important moment for the politicization of students. [...] The rejection of everything associated with the word "German" was part of a general opposition to German nationalism and appeared to be the logical conclusion of the confrontation with the history of National Socialism, its remnants and the half-hearted process of "coming to terms with the past."[210]

Yet, despite their rejection of National Socialism, a direct confrontation with nationalism did not occur. Nationalist positions were in fact existent in the New Left, though often repressed. The prominent student leader of 1968, Rudi Dutschke, advocated a "socialist reunification" of East and West Germany, positing a "connection between the national struggle and the class struggle," and sought to develop a "national self-consciousness."[211] He presented Germany as a victim of foreign aggression, and the East-West division as being disconnected from German aggression during World War Two. He was silent not only about the Holocaust but also about the role of the allied powers in liberating Germany from Nazism. Dutschke originally published these views under a pseudonym and only in the 1970s did he openly present these positions.

For many others of the New Left, an affirmative German national identity was blocked for many years. Yet, during this time, a "substitute nationalism" (*Ersatznationalismus*) had developed in the movement's support for national self-determination movements in the Global South. It was only later that the repressed object of national affirmation returned home, and German nationalism appeared again on the Left.[212]

In the 1980s, the lack of debate about nationalism eventually led to the embrace of multiculturalism as a response to rising German nationalism. Yet, this only affirmed cultural nationalism through the back door. "[T]he preoccupation with the nation," Ludwig writes, "does not rely upon recourse to loaded terms such as national pride and fatherland. With expressions such as 'collective identity' and with the category of culture, national meaning is just as easily transported."[213]

Against this background, the explicitly anti-national perspectives after 1989 represent a rupture with earlier traditions, and provide the beginnings of a new orientation. But what are the general contours of this anti-national perspective?

Although the campaigns *Never Again Germany!* and *Something Better than the Nation* were triggered by different aspects of resurgent nationalism—the Radical Left by geopolitical developments, and the *Wohlfahrtsausschüsse* by nationalism from below—both projects developed all-encompassing critiques targeting both state and civil society levels.

The *Never Again Germany!*-campaign focused on the geopolitical aspects of the new national consensus, opposing the reconstruction of political power and economic influence after the collapse of East Germany, and the attempts of an expanded West Germany to increase its role internationally. This shows a focus on the level of the nation-state and the increasing relevance of a national narrative for its political and economic pursuits.

The *Wohlfahrtsausschüsse* and the *Something Better than the Nation*-caravan on the other hand, concentrated on the spike in hostility and violence towards migrants in the early 1990s. They focused on the relationship between nationalism and racism from below and in the media, and their dynamic interplay with public policy (as, for example, with the abdication of asylum rights).

The *Never Again Germany!*-campaign, however, was not limited to a geopolitical critique: It also targeted the renationalization of civil society and societal consensus that made the political unification possible. That is to say, it focused on the domestic national consensus. In fact, Bernhard Schmid described this "ideological consensus" as "the point of departure of the 'anti-national' debate."[214]

Similarly, the work of the *Wohlfahrtsausschüsse* did not remain confined to the level of civil society. Instead, the group saw political events as playing a nurturing role for nationalism from below. Political unification and its accompanying national narrative provided impetus for hostility towards those viewed as outside of the national collectivity, and gave weight to patriarchal conceptions about how this collectivity should be organized internally.

But neither group stopped there. Not only did they draw out the connections between nationalism on state and civil society levels, providing an explanation of resurgent German nationalism as the result of conjunctural political factors (as, for example, of the reunification), they also saw nationalism as a central component of the normal functioning of capitalist society. For them, nationalism was not random or arbitrary, nor could it be disregarded as mere "false consciousness." Instead, nationalist positions derive from the structure of capitalist nation-states—with their competitive labor markets and international competition— which are made explicit, radicalized, and often racialized in concrete political contexts.[215] The struggle against nationalism therefore would also have to be directed against the basic structure of capitalist society from which nationalism springs.

## Against the Nation

The contours of an anti-national orientation for both the Radical Left and the Wohlfahrtsausschüsse is defined by an absolute, concrete, negative, universalism. The absolute rejection of the nation strongly contrasts to approaches centering upon the cultivation of a post-national, transnational or European identity. Instead of a strategy of gradual and expanding forms of inclusion, they opposed the nation outright, challenging its grounds of legitimation and of structural existence.

Neither mobilization sought to contain or humanize a German identity, or preserve it by routing out national "chauvinism" or "excesses." Nor did they defend a more "respectable" Germany against the nationalist frenzy, or attempt to preserve or protect it against "misuse." They did not long for a pre-1989 post-national collective identity, nor a pre-Nazi one.

While scattered references could be found that positively asserted West Germany's "multinational" character, or affirmed multiculturalism against an ethnically homogeneous national conception, such statements were marginal and largely absent from the projects' theoretical elucidations. (The only fleeting mention of such views is found in the short statement, "Thesis Paper on the Topic 'Ethnic-National Minorities.'"[216]) The dominant position did not propose or affirm an alternative collective identity. It was strictly negative in its approach.

This absolute rejection of the nation did not result in an over-identification with those subjects excluded or marginalized from national belonging. In other words, despite the practical and symbolic defense of asylum seekers and other migrants, these groups did not play the role of *ersatz* identity for a rejected German one, in the way that Latin American, Asian, African and Arab identities did for some segments of the New Left.

The anti-national critique was concrete in the sense that it did not emerge out of abstract theoretical considerations, but from struggles against actually existing forms of German nationalism in the political conjuncture after 1989. It was also concrete in the sense that the anti-national campaigns did not propose an abstract conception of humanity, but rather responded to acute societal threats as they were occurring.

They opposed the conceptual, practical and legal restrictions whereby nations were organized. This praxis of *negation* was directed at the actually existing national form as it presented itself, and against its radicalization and renewed ethnicization in the early 1990s. On the cultural level, it involved a deconstruction of cultural and historical narratives; on the state level, it meant opposing delimited citizenship rights, national borders and migration controls; and in the realm of civil society, it tried to counter physical violence and daily practices of exclusion.

Opposition on a structural level was seen in the *Never Again Germany!*-campaign's protest against the "Aliens Act" and other similar migration control policies by Germany and the EU, where they basically rejected any restrictions on migration or civil and political rights for those who lived in or desired to live in West Germany. The *Wohlfahrtsausschüsse* also expressed unconditional universalistic demands against the constitutional reform of asylum rights. Both of these examples show a negative universalism, against migration controls, national borders and the differentiated allotment of political rights.

This *concrete*, negative, universalist anti-nationalism is sharply contrasted to an *abstract*, universalist one, found in broad sections of the Left. Take for example, the autonomist theorist George Katsiaficas' approach to the topic.[217] In his book on the German and Italian autonomist movements, Katsiaficas criticizes the German autonomists for focusing on the particularities of *German* nationalism. In his view, such efforts only affirm it, and thereby obstruct the path towards the "universal species." To reach this goal, he claims, the contrary approach is required: Instead of identifying the particularities of German nationalism, one should "filter out the German dimension" and highlight universal human capacities.

In stark contrast to the anti-national perspective, which sees nationalism as a fundamentally modern phenomenon bound to capitalist society, this abstract, universalist position treats nationalism as a mere residue of pre-modern and pre-capitalist societies. According to Katsiaficas, it is nothing more than the "cultural remnants of tribalism and superstition" or "psychological remnants" which have yet to be transcended by civilizational progress.[218] While nationalism certainly has roots in pre-capitalist societal formations, this position fails to account for the ways nationalism is produced within capitalist societies as central ideological and structural components of their functioning.

The result of Katsiaficas' approach, like many of the participants in the autonomous movement themselves, was to downplay the rapidly increasing role of nationalism in the post-1989 period, or to reduce it to a problem of neo-fascism or racism.

In contrast to such an approach, the anti-nationalists intervened directly in the social-historical context and sought to disrupt its trajectory. This strongly contrasts with a tendency based on abstract universalism, which responded to nationalism by fleeing from, or denying association with, the particular German historical situation.

Indeed, the anti-national critique was directed precisely at *German* politics and history, in order to create a specifically *German* anti-national movement: One must, Maria Baader and Gotlinde Magiriba Lwanga insisted, "place oneself finally, as woman, as leftist, as German, as a white person, in the history," which specifically involved the recognition that nationalism, racism, and antisemitism "have a dynamic and a function which we have something to do with."[219] Therefore, to the activists of the *Never Again Germany!*-campaign, an anti-national position was not an abstraction, but a concrete reckoning with the social world one found oneself in. Following this logic, they explicitly sought "to create the basis for a *German anti-national movement*."[220]

In both campaigns, the anti-national perspective was not limited to a critique of exclusionary aspects of a delimited national collectivity, and particularly towards the exclusion of asylum seekers and non-German immigrants from this collective. Instead, they saw nationalism as having specific disadvantages even for some of those who belong to the nation. This we saw in the way the Radical Left addressed the rising levels of female unemployment following the privatization of East German industries, and their re-incorporation into the nation through unpaid domestic labor.

The nationalist narrative helped to rationalize this gendered division of labor and social segmentation, by presenting women not only as caretakers of the family but of the nation as a whole. This role allocation was supported by a patriarchal gender narrative and a national managerial position, which sought to ease the labor market of superfluous labor power in service of the national economy.

Class differences were also emphasized in the campaigns, arguing that low-wage workers would not see any of the economic benefits of political unification. "Modernization" under capitalist conditions involves polarization, yet societal consent for this project would be secured through a depiction of the nation as a horizontal community, of the belief that "we are all in the same boat."

The focus on nationalism's oppressive implications even for some of those included, marked a strong contrast to liberal theories of nationalism defined as inter-ethnic conflict. In contrast to this view, they saw nationalism as a central element for the production and reproduction of modern capitalist societies. This meant that they saw it as a phenomenon present at the levels of state and civil society, something that was used to justify public policy, racial violence and gender-role allocation, and for the construction of a national personal identity.

As seen in the *Never Again Germany!*-campaign, nationalism was viewed as the narrative component for an expanded German state, incorporating East Germany. In the projects of the *Wohlfahrtsausschüsse*, we saw how they understood national narratives as being used to justify forms of exclusion of those said to not belong to the "national community," whether that be by means of direct violence in civil society or by the mediated force of the state.

## Capitalism and the Nation-State

Participants of both campaigns saw the nation as a highly modern construct, rather than a transhistorical constant.[221] Sometimes directly citing the words of social theorist Benedict Anderson, they described nations as "imagined political communities."[222] Nations, they persistently argued, did not preclude modern nation-states, but were rather products of nationalism and of the nation-state.[223] Agreeing with Ernest Gellner and Karl Marx, nationalism was viewed as closely bound to the social order, even a result of it.[224] Nations are in fact products of nationalisms, and not the other way around.[225]

One sees also the influence of Eric Hobsbawm in their work when one reads his view of the nation. Not only did Hobsbawm agree with the modern theories of nationalism, and with the "element of artefact, invention and social engineering which enters into the making of nations,"[226] he also saw the role of nationalism and the nation-state in producing nations. He wrote:

> I do not regard the "nation" as a primary nor as an unchanging social entity. It belongs exclusively to a particular, and historically recent, period. It is a social entity only insofar as it relates to a certain kind of modern territorial state, the "nation-state," and it is pointless to discuss the nation and nationality except insofar as both relate to it. [...] In short, for the purpose of analysis nationalism comes before nations. Nations do not make states and nationalisms but the other way around.[227]

The central role of capitalism within modern nation-states occupied a critical role in the anti-nationalists' views on nationalism. For them, the competitive logic of capitalist society was seen as a main source for the development of nationalism, both on the internal, domestic level of competition between individuals on the labor market, as well as between nation-states on the international level. This competition is "ethnicized," and the state is drawn upon by the populace to preserve or to give advantages to the "national community" from which the state draws its legitimacy.

As the nation is "inherently limited,"[228] these movements refused this delimited collectivity and the differential allotment of political rights. As a result of their view of the bounded relationship between nationalism, the nation and the nation-state, the response to nationalism resulted in the rejection of the nation-state as a specific form of political rule, and not only to oppose nationalism as a form of "excessive" national feeling.

## The Left and the People

In view of broad public approval for political unification, the anti-national movement was deeply estranged from the German civilian population. Yet, as verbal and physical attacks on minorities skyrocketed in the early 1990s, this relationship became one of increasing conflict.

Whereas social movements often hold an affirmative attitude towards "society" against the state—just as labor movements affirm workers against capital—the post-1989 national consensus threw this orientation into disarray. The "masses" were not simply passive victims of capitalism, but were active in its making, and in some cases, of deeply reactionary turns. Reactionary politics can emerge from below. With this observation, how should the Left respond?

For participants of these two campaigns, the general population was seen not as a mere object ruled over by the state, but as a conglomeration of subjects pushing for or approving of certain social and political developments. For the anti-national groups, it became less a force to be mobilized, and increasingly one to be opposed. This was most clear in the case of the *Never Again Germany!*-campaign, based on a strategy of building a counter-power from within left-wing social movements to the political unification and its supporters within the population.

In the case of the *Wohlfahrtsausschüsse*, the relation to the population was more complicated. Originally, they employed a strategy of cultural intervention, supporting people in East Germany towards the construction of a public force in opposition to the resurgent Right. Yet, their conclusion that this endeavor was a complete failure—that the German population was indifferent, if not actively involved, in the pogroms against asylum seekers, foreign contract workers, and other "non-Germans"—created deep mistrust towards the population, which would strongly influence Left projects in the future. The German public came to be seen, in some sense, as a hindrance to progressive or emancipatory aims and as an object of critique and opposition.

With the campaigns against nationalism in the early 1990s, we witnessed the development of an approach that not only opposed nationalism, but also rejected the concept of the nation and the political formation of the nation-state.

The campaigns marked the beginning of an anti-national praxis. Targeting different aspects of the new "national consensus" since the fall of the Berlin Wall, they produced novel perspectives that broke with previous approaches to the topics of nationalism, the nation and the nation-state.[229]

## The Global Economic Crisis Today

Immediately following the financial meltdown of 2007/2008, nationalist movements were on the rise. In Germany, the populist "Pro-Germany" movements gained broader appeal with the help of centrist political leaders who blamed immigration for the supposed downfall of the country. The finance minister of Berlin and chairman of the German Central Bank, the Social Democratic Party's Thilo Sarrazin, accused Turkish and Muslim communities in Germany of bringing about economic and cultural ruin.

As Greece became caught in the crisis, the German press began a media campaign targeting the supposed cultural characteristics of southern Europeans. Against all statistical facts, Greeks were said to be working too little, vacationing too much, and going into retirement too early.[230] This followed the German government's crisis management strategy at the European Union level, forcing drastic austerity measures upon the population of the southern European state, limiting popular democratic rights, and installing technocratic leaders.

In Norway, this anti-immigrant and social chauvinistic line erupted in direct violence, when Anders Behring Breivik opened fire on youth attending a summer camp of the Norwegian Labor Party. The influence upon the social democratic party by "cultural Marxism"—usually a code word for the Jewish Left—was apparently behind its supposed support for multiculturalism and liberal immigration policies, responsible for the downfall of Christian Europe.

England has also seen its nationalist response to the crisis, with the slogan "British Jobs for British Workers!" appearing in demonstrations by striking construction workers, protesting multinational corporations for wage dumping through the use of foreign labor. While it was Right-wing activists who brought the slogan into the labor struggle, it originates with British Prime Minister Gordon Brown. He was seeking to win conservative voters back to his party who had drifted to the far-Right, and to push British nationals off the "dole" by offering them employment privileges above other European workers.

The United States has also experienced the rebirth of nationalism with the populist Tea Party movement, which blames the recession on demographic shifts and the Obama Presidency. As a result, the victims of the crisis should pay again, this time through cuts to unemployment aid, welfare, and public education, and with the revocation of Obama's healthcare reforms.

The movement's political demands for neoliberal austerity reveal a color line, in which existing material benefits for whites would be protected while those for people of color would be reduced. For example, they advocate that the cuts should not apply to government healthcare and retirement programs disproportionately supporting white retirees.[231] In some cases, the element of white backlash within the Tea Party movement was made explicit, for example, when its popular television leader, Glenn Beck, characterized efforts to extend healthcare coverage to the millions of uninsured people as "reparations for slavery."[232]

In fact, the source of the problem according to Tea Party activists is that the President is not a "real" American. For proponents of the "birther" conspiracy—a view shared by over 60% of Republicans[233]—Obama is fabricating his U.S. birth-certificate to cover up his "real" birthplace in Kenya. This focus on "real America" has a strong cultural component. As Sarah Palin and many other conservatives propagate, Obama supposedly holds foreign values, more in line with European socialism than with American free-enterprise.

Some participants of the *Occupy* movement gloss over the nationalist politics of the Tea Party movement, seeing in its supposed anti-government rebellion, the seeds of a progressive movement. *Adbusters* envisioned an *Occupy* movement that would "transcend" the Tea Party and not directly confront it. Similarly, the US Day of Rage called on "the nation" to rebel against "the elite," to reclaim "American institutions" from their usurpation by "oligarchs" and "cleptocrats," and echoing the conservative Right, to "take the country back" and restore America as a "great nation."

The global movements of 2011, beginning in Tunisia and Egypt, erupting in Spain, Greece, and Portugal, spreading across the Atlantic to the United States, inspiring widespread student strikes in Chile and massive protests in Israel, reveals the potential for a global Left resurgence. But these mobilizations also possess the danger of reaffirming the national framework as a strategy to "solve" the global crisis. It must therefore develop ways of seeing this threat, critiquing its particular expressions in distinct contexts, and countering it with concrete political projects.

The difficulty is that nationalism is easy to detect when it is expressed in explicit ethnic or racial terms, and difficult to grasp when it comes in cultural forms or in the language of "society." For example, the dominant form that everyday nationalism takes today is through what Joachim Hirsch calls the "national competitive state." By this he means the state's efforts to "mobilize all productive forces for the purposes of international competition."[234]

It was precisely this form of nationalism that the Radical Left targeted when it criticized how unpaid domestic labor was being developed as a solution to rising female unemployment following the privatization of the East German economy. In this situation, all productive forces would be mobilized in service of the national economy.

But insofar as the national economy lacked the capacity at that time to productively absorb the entire employable population towards these ends, the public was segmented along gender lines. Its re-organization according to the needs of the "national competitive state" was ideologically justified by presenting women not only as the caretakers of the family, but of the larger collective, the nation.

This kind of process is a regular part of capitalist societies today, and present in crisis management strategies in many national contexts, even without recourse to explicit ethnic or racial terms.

A contemporary example of this is the politics of the current U.S. president. Obama is not often associated with nationalism, yet his public addresses are deeply based in a strategy of the national competitive state. During the tax debates in Washington in 2010, in which Obama warred with Republicans, he warned a group of college students against "partisanship" and "politics." Instead, he advanced the idea of the collective interests of Americans across political persuasions.

There is a "common need" to make the United States more economically competitive on the international market, he argued and warned that country is "in danger of falling behind in the global economy." There is "fierce competition among nations for the jobs and industries of the future" which threatens America of being "out-paced by up and coming competitors like China and India."[235] Obama said:

> In the twentieth century, the business of America was business. Our economic leadership in the world went unmatched. Now it's up to us to make sure that we maintain that leadership in this century. And at this moment, the most important contest we face is not between Democrats and Republicans. It's between America and our economic competitors all around the world. That's the competition we've got to spend time thinking about.[236]

In this short statement, Obama demonstrates just how closely connected the affirmation of the national competitive state is with the subordination of political and class conflicts. As Paul Street shows, Obama's speech reveals his "belief that the dictates of the market [...] must trump the odious twaddle of (what passes for) democratic debate and contestation."[237] According to this conception, "petty and silly partisanship and angry 'politics,'" and pressuring for "progressive taxation," is "counter-productive."[238]

What is needed is for "all good market-based Americans to pull together in a big common effort to maintain national capitalist leverage in flat-world competition with low-wage information workers in India and China we have been pitted against by the march of globalization."[239]

While Street clearly shows how Obama's nationalist rhetoric goes hand in hand with his silence on class and material conflicts, he does so through a deep personalization of the issues, focusing largely on Obama's character.[240]

It is here that the 2009 Social Revolutionary and Antinational Bloc in Germany might be instructive. In contrast to Street's approach, the Bloc did not target Lafontaine's migration policies as the product of merely private views, but rather, as the logical outcome of a politics subordinated to the nation-state. Without opposing global capitalist competition, the state comes to the forefront for advancing national interests and the national economy. This requires appealing to the common identity of the national citizens, pitting them against non-nationals, and pinning the improvement of their material situations to the national economy's success on the global market. In short, emancipation from capitalist society could not be achieved without combating nationalism and abolishing the nation-state.

But this provides no easy recipe for anti-capitalist movements either in Germany or elsewhere.

The anti-national campaigns of the early 1990s broke with the Left's inherited positions on nationalism. The new movement rejected the romantic notion of "the people" and the affirmation of the "nation" as the force of emancipation. This marked a rupture with the Old Left's proletarian internationalism and the New Left's support for national self-determination movements.

Yet, despite their deep mistrust of the German population in the political conjuncture of reunification, they did not simply invert the romantic and affirmative national perspective. That is, neither the *Never Again Germany!* nor the *Something Better than the Nation* campaigns demonized German society in a crude and universal way. Instead, they explicitly targeted nationalism from below, and the population's role in regressive social and political developments.

While they also sharply criticized the German state, they did not produce a singular position on the state as such, nor on how anti-capitalist movements should relate to it. Unlike the Social Revolutionary and Anti-National Bloc in 2009, who rejected the state wholesale—believing it to be submerged completely under the total subordination of capital—the movement of the early 1990s did not advance a non-statist alternative. Their praxis was wholly negative, targeting particular policies and the general trends of the newly expanded, increasingly powerful, and nationalistic German state at that time.

While I have shown how some sections of the German Left responded to resurgent nationalism since 1989, this book is motivated by failures of the U.S. left to grapple with nationalism within the movement and society. By illuminating some parts of the history of the German anti-national Left, I hope to raise the level of knowledge about the ways they respond to different forms of nationalism, to increase international dialogue on the topic, and to bring some potential insights to the necessary debates elsewhere.

This process does not imply the simple adoption of positions developed in Germany by leftists in other national contexts. Instead I hope to have provided insights into a particular Left attempt to analyze and confront the connections between nationalism and capitalism. My hope is that this book might encourage anti-capitalists elsewhere to face new difficult questions, which could lead to productive pathways towards an emancipatory society, beyond capitalism, the state, and the nation.

# NOTES

*All translations from German to English have been done by Robert Ogman, unless otherwise noted.*

1. Der sozialrevolutionäre und antinationale Block, "Lafontaine Rede ist eine Provokation!" March 2009 (Available at antifa-frankfurt.org).

2. Der sozialrevolutionäre und antinationale Block, "Das Ei ist rund damit das Denken die Richtung ändern kann. Autonome Antifa verteidigt Eierwürfe auf Lafontaine und kritisiert Nationalismus," March 2009 (Available at antifa-frankfurt.org).

3. Ibid.

4. Ibid.

5. Ibid.

6. Throughout this book a "nation" is taken to be an "imaginary community," a modern phenomenon born with the emergence

of capitalist society. This is both a basic assumption of this book and a common denominator of the anti-national tendency, even as actors within this milieu drew from other theories to sharpen and specify their analyses. Throughout the book, where the term "nation" is used, it will always be regarded as an "imaginary community" brought into existence by certain social and material conditions and never as a natural fact divorced from them. See Benedict Anderson, *Imagined Communities* (London: Verso, 2002).

7. The incorporation of the former territory of the German Democratic Republic into the Federal Republic of Germany in 1989/1990 is termed "German reunification." The term however, clearly gives positive normative meaning to this political event, and presents it as a logical process of the natural coming together of a divided nation. Former Social Democratic mayor of West Berlin, Willy Brandt, perfectly expresses this political sentiment in his statement about the opening of the Berlin Wall: "now grows together what belongs together" ("Jetzt wächst zusammen, was zusammengehört"). Because an alternative, critical term has not been found to describe this political process, this book will sometimes use the dominant term "reunification" which will not always be placed in quotation marks. Like the term "the nation," the reader should understand the author's critical distance towards these terms even when they are not placed in quotation marks. As we will see, the naturalization of these terms is strongly contested by the anti-national Left.

8. Anti-Fascist Forum, *My Enemy's Enemy: Essays on Globalization, Fascism and the Struggle against Capitalism* (Montreal: Kersplebedeb, 2001).

9. On nationalism and antisemitism in the anti-globalization

movement, see Werner Bonefeld "Nationalism and Anti-Semitism in Anti-Globalization Perspective" in Werner Bonefeld and Kosmas Psychopedis (eds.), *Human Dignity: Social Autonomy and the Critique of Capitalism* (Ashgate: Hants England, 2005).

10. For a critique of "neo anti-imperialism," its similarities with right-wing positions, and its non-emancipatory character, see Moishe Postone, "History and Helplessness: Mass Mobilization and Contemporary Forms of Anticapitalism," *Public Culture* 18:1 (2006), 93-110.

11. See Peter Hudis, "Resistance or Retrogression? The Battle of Ideas over Iraq," *News and Letters*, November 2004.

12. Judith Butler, "On Hamas, Hezbollah & the Israel Lobby," 2006 (Available at radicalarchives.org).

13. Uncritical support for Iran's President Ahmadinejad was shown in the attendance by leftists of his meetings in New York City, and their silence regarding Iran's repression of demonstrators and social justice activists. See Bitta Mostofi, "We're Better Than This. Admiring Ahmadinejad and Overlooking Activists," *Counterpunch*, October 15-17, 2010, and the editorial, "U.S. progressives meet with Iranian President Mahmoud Ahmadinejad," *FightBackNews*, October 23, 2010.

14. See Alexander Cockburn, "25 Years After Vietnam: Beyond Left and Right," in *Counterpunch,* April 14-16, 2000.

15. Alison Weir, "The New 'Blood Libel'? Israeli Organ Harvesting," *Counterpunch*, August 28-30, 2009. For a critique, see Adam Holland, "Blood Libel Promoted By Counterpunch," September 11, 2009 (Available at adamholland.blogspot.com).

16. Michael Neumann, "What Is Antisemitism?" *Counterpunch,* June 4, 2002. In the article Neumann continues: "This is not

to excuse genuine anti-Semitism; it is to trivialize it" and "Undoubtedly there is genuine antisemitism in the Arab world: the distribution of the Protocols of the Elders of Zion, the myths about stealing the blood of gentile babies. This is utterly inexcusable. So was your failure to answer Aunt Bee's last letter." Not only does he aim to trivialize antisemitism, he also actively promotes it. In an exchange with the openly antisemitic website *Jewish Tribal Review* he differentiates between "good" and "bad" antisemites, and expresses his lack of concern that Nazis and racists use his material. This is documented in David Hirsch, "How Anti-Zionism lays the basis for open antisemitism," *Engage*, June 7, 2005.

17. On their "Who We Are" page the editors explain that they "represent the truly pro-America side of the foreign policy debate." They are "real American patriots." They continue in the tradition of the right-wing anti-interventionist "America First Committee!" of the 1940s. Their previous political involvement was in the Libertarian Republican Organizing Committee and they seek to "go beyond Left and Right."

18. See for example Robert Fisk, "The United States of Israel," *Counterpunch*, April 27, 2006, and James Petras, *The Power of Israel in the United States* (Atlanta: Clarity Press, 2006). Also see the critical review by Allen Ruff, "Do Zionists Run America?" *Against the Current* 128, May-June 2007 (Available at solidarity-us.org). Ruff focuses on the role of populism in Petras' text, which presents an otherwise healthy U.S. body politic being usurped by foreign agents. The book supports a populism with "a penchant for conspiratorial theory and a related quest to exorcize evil cabals, rid the country of outsiders and/or their domestic agents and reclaim 'the republic.'"

19. John Mearsheimer and Stephen Walt, *The Israel Lobby and U.S. Foreign Policy* (Farrar, Straus and Giraux: New York, 2007), originally published as an essay, "The Israel Lobby," *London Review of Books*, Vol. 28, No. 6 (March 23, 2006), 3-12.

20  Noam Chomsky, "The Israel Lobby?" *ZNet*, March 28, 2006, emphasis added.

21. Ibid.

22. See Kalle Lasn, "Elliott Abrams, Dual Loyalist and Neocon Extraordinaire," *Adbusters* 74, September 28, 2007.

23. James Kirchick, "A case of leftist 'McCarthyism'?" *Ha'aretz*, January 13, 2012.

24. Mearsheimer and Walt advocate a U.S. grand strategy of "offshore balancing" with limited military involvement, in which the U.S.'s "principal goal" is to ensure that "no country dominates" the three strategically important regions—Europe, Northeast Asia and the Persian Gulf—"as it [the U.S.] dominates the Western hemisphere." In this way, "dangerous rivals in other regions are forced to concentrate their attention on great powers in their own backyards rather than be free to interfere in America's." They continue: "The best way to achieve that end is to rely on local powers to counter aspiring regional hegemons and otherwise keep U.S. military forces over the horizon. But if that improves impossible, American troops come from offshore to help do the job, and then leave once the potential hegemon is checked." See John J. Mearsheimer, "Imperial by Design," *The National Interest* 11 (Jan/Feb 2011), 18.

25. Bill Weinberg, "The Israel Lobby and Global Hegemony: Revisited. The Mearsheimer-Walt Thesis Deconstructed," *WW4Report*, September 1, 2007.

26. Seth Weiss, "Wall Street Protests Marred by Anti-Semitism,"

*Marxist Humanist Initiative*, October 5, 2011.

27. Joseph Berger, "Cries of Anti-Semitism, but Not at Zuccotti Park," *New York Times* October 21, 2011.

28. Kalle Lasn, "Why Won't Anyone Say They Are Jewish?" *Adbusters*, March/April 2004.

29. Editorial, "#Occupywallstreet. A shift in revolutionary tactics," *Adbusters*, July 13, 2011.

30. Editorial, "Planned Protests for #Sept17 #occupywallstreet #usdor," *US Day of Rage*, August 27, 2011.

31. On right-wing participation in the Occupy movement, see: Spencer Sunshine, "Occupied with Conspiracies?" *Shift*, November 2011; Matthew Lyons, "Rightists woo the Occupy Wall Street Movement," *ThreeWayFight*, November 8, 2011; and Matthew Lyons "Occupy movement: Anti-capitalism versus populism," *ThreeWayFight*, December 6, 2011.

32. G.B. Taylor, "Form als Fetisch," *Phase-Zwei* No. 41 (Winter 2011/12).

33. For a detailed description of the first weeks and months of organizing see David Graeber, *Inside Occupy* (Frankfurt and New York: Campus, 2012).

34. Anti-Fascist Forum, *My Enemy's Enemy*.

35. Don Hammerquist, J. Sakai, ARA Chicago, and Mark Salotte, *Confronting Fascism: Discussion Documents for a Militant Movement* (Chicago and Montreal: ARA Chicago, Kersplebedeb, Arsenal, 2002).

36. Eric Krebbers and Merijn Schoenmaker, "De Fabel van de Illegaal Quits Dutch Anti-MAI Campaign," in Anti-Fascist Forum, *My Enemy's Enemy*, 62.

37. Ibid., 62.

38. Ibid., 67.

39.  Ibid., 62, emphasis added.

40.  Ibid., 67.

41.  Eric Krebbers, Harry Westerink and Merijn Schoenmaker, "Fabel Self-Interview about Quitting with the Campaigns Against 'Free Trade'," in Anti-Fascist Forum, *My Enemy's Enemy*, 88.

42.  Ibid., 89.

43.  Eric Krebbers and Merijn Schoenmaker, "Campaign Against the MAI Potentially Antisemitic," in Anti-Fascist Forum, *My Enemy's Enemy*, 71.

44.  Krebbers, Westerink and Schoenmaker, "Fabel Self-Interview," 89.

45.  Krebbers and Schoenmaker, "Campaign Against the MAI Potentially Antisemitic," in Anti-Fascist Forum, *My Enemy's Enemy*, 71.

46.  Hildeyard quoted in Krebbers and Schoenmaker, "De Fabel van de Illegaal Quits Dutch Anti-MAI Campaign," 67.

47.  See Lyons, "Rightists woo the Occupy Wall Street movement."

48.  Michael Staudenmaier, "Anti-Semitism, Islamophobia, and the Three Way Fight," *Upping the Anti* 5 (October 2007).

49.  Ibid.

50.  Ibid.

51.  Matthew Lyons, "Defending my Enemy's Enemy," *ThreeWayFight*, August 3, 2006.

52.  Staudenmaier, "Anti-Semitism, Islamophobia, and the Three Way Fight."

53.  For more on the "concretization of the abstract" as "a fetishization of capital on the global level as the USA, or, in some variants, as the USA and Israel" in the "neo-anti-imperialism," see Moishe Postone, "History and Helplessness."

54.  Stephen Padgett, William E. Paterson and Gordon Smith, *Developments in German Politics 3* (New York: Palgrave

Macmillan, 2003), 11.

55.   Ibid., 11.

56.   Ibid., 14, emphasis in original.

57.   Ibid., 11.

58.   Michael Binyon, "Thatcher told Gorbachev Britain did not
      want German Reunification," *Times Online*, September 11,
      2009, and Carsten Volkery, "The Iron Lady's Views on German
      Reunification," *Der Spiegel Online*, September 11, 2009.

59.   Ibid.

60.   Padgett et al., *Developments in German Politics*, 10.

61.   Ibid., 10.

62.   Hans Kundnani, *Utopia or Auschwitz: Germany's 1968 Generation
      and the Holocaust*, (London: Hurst C & Co Publishers Ltd.,
      2009); and Norbert Frei, *1968: Jugendrevolte und Globaler Protest*
      (Munich: Deutscher Taschenbuch Verlag, 2008), 79-88.

63.   Two examples from the 1980s were the Bitburg incident and
      the Historians' Dispute. The Bitburg incident was the meeting
      between German Chancellor Helmut Kohl and U.S. President
      Ronald Reagan in 1985 at the graves of SS soldiers at the military
      cemetery in Bitburg, in which a symbolic reconciliation took
      place. The Historian's Dispute involved the attempt amongst
      conservative historians to rehabilitate the period of National
      Socialism by portraying the Third Reich as a mere response to,
      and a defense against, Stalinism and the Soviet Union.

64.   Paul Hockenos, *Free to Hate: The Rise of the Right in Post-
      Communist Eastern Europe*, (New York: Routledge, 1992), 42.

65.   Jürgen Habermas, "Der DM-Nationalismus," *Die Zeit*, March
      30, 1990.

66.   Ibid.

67.   Günter Grass, "Rede des Schriftstellers Günter Grass auf dem

Parteitag der SPD in Berlin, 18.12.1989," in Peter Alter, ed., *Nationalismus: Dokumente zur Geschichte und Gegenwart eines Phänomens* (Munich: Serie Piper, 1994), 301.

68. *Grundgesetz der Bundesrepublik Deutschland*, (Berlin: Deutscher Bundestag, 2009), Art. 116.

69. This principle is contrasted to that of *ius soli*—practiced in many European countries—which grants citizenship to all those born within the state's territory, regardless of ancestry.

70. Simon Green, "Towards an Open Society? Citizenship and Immigration," in Padgett et al., *Developments in German Politics*, 245.

71. Ibid., 245.

72. Ibid., 230.

73. *Grundgesetz*, Art. 16a.

74. Green, "Towards an Open Society?" 234.

75. Ibid., 232-233.

76. Karen Schönwälder, "Migration, Refugees, and Ethnic Plurality as Issues of Public and Political Debates in (West) Germany," in David Cesarani and Mary Fulbrook (eds.), *Citizenship, Nationality and Migration in Europe* (London and New York: Routledge, 1997), 160.

77. Ibid., 160.

78. Ibid., 159-160.

79. Roger Karapin, *Protest Politics in Germany: Movements on the Left and Right Since the 1960s* (Pennsylvania: Penn State Press, 2007), 194-195.

80. Ibid., 194.

81. Ibid., 194-195.

82. Ibid., 210-211.

83. Ibid., 217.

84. Schönwälder, "Migration, Refugees, and Ethnic Plurality," 178.

85. Roland Roth and Dietrich Rucht (eds.), *Die sozialen Bewegungen in Deutschland seit 1945* (Frankfurt: Campus, 2008), 142.

86. Hermann Kurthen, Werner Bergmann, and Rainer Erb (eds.), *Antisemitism and Xenophobia in Germany after Unification* (New York: Oxford University Press, 1997), 8.

87. Ibid., 8.

88. Ibid., 8.

89. Ibid., 8.

90. Ibid., 8.

91. Ibid., 8.

92. Ibid., 8.

93. Ibid., 8.

94. Aslan Erkol and Nora Winter, "Chronik der Gewalt: 182 Todesopfer rechtsextremer und rassistischer Gewalt seit 1990," *Mut Gegen Rechte Gewalt*, November 23, 2011.

95. Green, "Towards an Open Society?" 235.

96. Ibid., 235.

97. Kongressvorbereitungsgruppe (eds.), *Die Radikale Linke. Reader zum Kongress*, (Hamburg: Konkret Literatur Verlag, 1990).

98. Kongressvorbereitungsgruppe (eds.), *"Deutschland? Nie Wieder!" Kongress der Radikalen Linken*, (Köln and Karlsruhe: ISP, 1990).

99. Kongressvorbereitungsgruppe (eds.), *Die Radikale Linke*, 1990, 11.

100. Ibid., 30.

101. Ibid., 11-30.

102. Ibid., 12.

103. Kongressvorbereitungsgruppe (eds.), *"Deutschland? Nie Wieder!"* 235-239.

104. Gerber, *Nie Wieder Deutschland?* 103.

105. Ibid., 130.

106. Ibid., 103.

107. Gaston Kirsche, "Hypermarginalisierte Outlaws," *Konkret* 2 (2003), 24.

108. Winfried Wolf, "Schweigen, weil das vierte Reich ohnehin kommt?" in Kongressvorbereitungsgruppe (eds.), *Die Radikale Linke. Reader zum Kongress*, 8.

109. Ibid., 8.

110. Ibid., 9.

111. Kongressvorbereitungsgruppe (eds.) *"Deutschland? Nie Wieder!"* 128.

112. Ibid., 128.

113. Ibid., 128.

114. Ibid., 128.

115. Ibid., 124-128.

116. Hamide Scheer, "Redebeitrag auf dem Kongress der Radikalen Linken," in Kongressvorbereitungsgruppe (eds.), *"Deutschland? Nie Wieder!" Kongress der Radikalen Linken* (Köln and Karlsruhe: ISP, 1990), 25-26.

117. Detlev zum Winkel, "Deutsche Frage—welche Frage?" in Kongressvorbereitungsgruppe (eds.), *"Deutschland? Nie Wieder!"* 197.

118. Radikale Linke, "Nie Wieder Deutschland! Erklärung gegen »Wieder-« und »Neuvereinigung« von BRD und DDR, 21.1.1990," in Kongressvorbereitungsgruppe (eds.), *Die Radikale Linke*, 193-198.

119. Die Radikale Linke,*"Deutschland? Nie Wieder!"* 193.

120. Ibid., 195.

121. The Council for Mutual Economic Assistance was an organization for economic cooperation between Eastern Block countries and in the Soviet Union's sphere of influence.

122. Die Radikale Linke, *"Deutschland? Nie Wieder!"* 195.

123. Ibid., 195.

124. Angelika Beer et al., "Gegen die Kolonisierung der osteuropäischen Staaten durch BRD, EG und NATO!" in Kongressvorbereitungsgruppe (eds.), *Die Radikale Linke*, 31.

125. Ibid., 34.

126. Ibid., 34.

127. Ibid., 35.

128. Thomas Ebermann, Georg Fülberth and Hermann L. Gremliza, "Rechts ist die deutsche Mitte," in Kongressvorbereitungsgruppe (eds.), *Die Radikale Linke*, 74.

129. Ibid., 74.

130. Ibid., 74.

131. Anderson, *Imagined Communities*, 7.

132. Ebermann et al., "Rechts ist die deutsche Mitte," 77.

133. Wolf, "Schweigen, weil das vierte Reich ohnehin kommt?," 9.

134. Die Radikale Linke, *Grundlagen der Radikalen Linken*, 20.

135. Hermann Gremliza, "Rede auf dem Kongress der Radikalen Linke," in Kongressvorbereitungsgruppe (eds.), *"Deutschland? Nie Wieder!"* 33.

136. Ibid., 33.

137. Ibid., 33.

138. Ibid., 33.

139. Bernhard Schmid, "Deutschland Reise auf die 'Bahamas': Vom Produkt der Linken zur neo-autoritären Sekte," in Gerhard Hanloser (ed.), *"Sie warn die Antideutschesten der deutschen Linken": Zu Geschichte, Kritik und Zukunft antideutscher Politik* (Münster: Unrast, 2004), 26.

140. Ibid., 26.

141. Zum Winkel, "Deutsche Frage—welche Frage?" 194.

142. Ibid., 194.

143. Ebermann et al., "Rechts ist die deutsche Mitte," 74.

144. Ibid., 74.

145. Ibid., 74

146. Ibid., 78.

147. Ibid., 78-79.

148. Ibid., 78-79.

149. Ibid., 79.

150. Ibid., 79.

151. Ibid., 78.

152. Ibid., 74.

153. Die Radikale Linke, *Die Radikale Linke*, 197.

154. Ibid., 197.

155. Ibid., 197.

156. FreundInnenkreis der Radikalen Linken, Köln, "Thesenpapier zum Thema 'Ethnisch-nationale Minderheiten,'" in Kongressvorbereitungsgruppe (eds.), *"Deutschland? Nie Wieder!"* 166.

157. Ibid., 166.

158. Gaston Kirsche, "Hypermarginalisierte Outlaws," in *Konkret* 2 (2003), 24.

159. Maria Baader and Gotlinde Magiriba Lwanga, "Redebeitrag auf dem Kongress der Radikalen Linken," in Kongressvorbereitungsgruppe (eds.), *"Deutschland? Nie Wieder!"* 24, emphasis in original.

160. Anderson, *Imagined Communities*, 7.

161. Wohlfahrtsausschuss Hamburg, "Unser Minimalziel," in Wohlfahrtsausschüsse (eds.), *Etwas Besseres als die Nation. Materialien zur Abwehr des gegenrevolutionären Übels*, (Berlin and Amsterdam: Edition ID-Archiv, 1994), 17.

162. Wohlfahrtsausschuss Hamburg, "Etwas Besseres als die Nation: Zur Begründung der Tour" in Wohlfahrtsausschüsse (eds.),

*Etwas Besseres als die Nation*, 46.

163. Wohlfahrtsausschuss Hamburg, "Unser Minimalziel," 17-18.

164. Ibid., 17.

165. Ibid., 17.

166. Ibid., 17.

167. Ibid., 18.

168. Wohlfahrtsausschüsse (eds.), *Etwas Besseres als die Nation*, 13.

169. Ibid., 13.

170. Wohlfahrtsausschuss Hamburg, "Unser Minimalzeil," 18.

171. Wohlfahrtsausschuss Hamburg, "Zur Begründung der Tour," 45, emphasis in original.

172. Ibid., 45.

173. Ibid., 47.

174. Ibid., 46.

175. Ibid., 48.

176. Ibid., 47.

177. Ibid., 47.

178. Wohlfahrtsausschüsse (eds.), *Etwas Besseres als die Nation*, v.

179. Andreas Fanizadeh, "Vorwort," in Wohlfahrtsausschüsse (eds.), *Etwas Besseres als die Nation*, 7.

180. Ibid., 7.

181. Ibid., 7-8.

182. Ibid., 7-8.

183. Ibid., 9.

184. Wohlfahrtsausschuss Hamburg, "Zur Begründung der Tour," 47.

185. Ibid., 47.

186. Ibid., 47.

187. Wohlfahrtsausschuss Frankfurt am Main/Autonomes Antirassistisches Plenum Frankfurt am Main, "Neue Hausordnung: Betreten Verboten!" in Wohlfahrtsausschüsse

(eds.), *Etwas Besseres als die Nation. Materialien zur Abwehr des gegenrevolutionären Übels.* (Berlin and Amsterdam: Edition ID-Archiv, 1994), 163.

188. Wolf Wetzel, "Die Abschaffung des Asylrechts 1993—ein Rückblick," *EyesWideShut*, January 20, 2008.

189. Ibid.

190. Ibid.

191. Autonome l.u.p.u.s.-Gruppe, "Gegen die völkische Mitte," in Wohlfahrtsausschüsse (eds.), *Etwas Besseres als die Nation*, 33.

192. Ibid., 32.

193. Ibid., 34, emphasis in original.

194. Wohlfahrtsausschuss Hamburg, "Etwas Besseres als die Nation," 45.

195. Wohlfahrtsausschuss Frankfurt am Main/Autonomes Antirassistisches Plenum Frankfurt am Main, "Neue Hausordnung," 163.

196. Terkessidis, "Die Geschichte zurückerobern," 80.

197. Ibid., 80.

198. Wohlfahrtsausschuss Hamburg, "Etwas Besseres als die Nation," 48.

199. Ibid., 48.

200. Günther Jacob, "Ich-Identität und nationale Identität," in Wohlfahrtsausschüsse (eds.), *Etwas Besseres als die Nation*, 70.

201. Wohlfahrtsausschuss Hamburg, "Etwas Besseres als die Nation," 50.

202. Ibid., 49.

203. Ibid., 50.

204. Ibid., 50.

205. Ibid., 50.

206. Ibid., 50.

207. Günther Jacob, "Ich-Identität und nationale Identität," 62.

208. Ibid., 48.

209. Andrea Ludwig, "Die 'Neue Linke' und die Nation: Über

den linken Umgang mit dem Eigenen und dem Fremden," in Guiseppe Orsi et al. (eds.), *Rechtsphilosophische Hefte*, Vol. 3 (Frankfurt AM: Peter Lang, 1994), 104.

210. Ibid., 104.

211. Kundnani, *Utopia or Auschwitz*, 149.

212. Ludwig, "Die 'Neue Linke' und die Nation," 100.

213. Ibid., 103.

214. Schmid, "Deutschland Reise auf die 'Bahamas,'" 29.

215. This topic would eventually become a central debate within the movement. On the one hand, anti-national critique was aimed at understanding the normal presence of nationalism as a central component of capitalist society, which becomes prominent at particular political conjunctures. On the other hand, the historical attempt of the National Socialist regime to establish a "Volksgemeinschaft" (a blood and soil racial community), reveals the capacity of nationalist movements to break with critical aspects of capitalism, instituting racialized, authoritarian societies.

216. FreundInnenkreis der Radikalen Linken, Köln, "Thesenpapier," 166.

217. George Katsiaficas, *The Subversion of Politics: European Autonomous Social Movements And The Decolonization Of Everyday Life* (Oakland: AK Press, 2006).

218. Ibid., 181.

219. Baader and Lwanga, "Redebeitrag," 24.

220. Ibid., 24, emphasis in original.

221. See Ernst Gellner, *Nations and Nationalism* (Ithaca: Cornell University Press, 2008), 6, and Eric J. Hobsbawm, *Nations and Nationalism Since 1780: Programme, Myth, Reality* (Cambridge, UK: Cambridge University Press, 1997), 9.

222. Anderson, *Imagined Communities*, 6.

223. Gellner, *Nations and Nationalism*, 54.

224. Ibid., xxii.

225. Ibid., xxii.

226. Hobsbawm, *Nations and Nationalism Since 1780*, 10.

227. Ibid., 9-10.

228. Anderson, *Imagined Communities*, 6.

229. See Ludwig, "Die 'Neue Linke' und die Nation," 103-117.

230. This cultural nationalist campaign and the actual roots of the crisis, are explained in Stephan Kaufmann, Antonella Muzzupappa, and Sabine Nuss, "'Sell Your Islands, You Bankrupt Greeks': 20 Popular Fallacies Concerning the Euro Crisis," (Berlin: Rosa Luxemburg Stiftung, 2011).

231. See Chronic Condition Data Warehouse, "Medicare Enrollment by Race, 1999-2009" (http://www.ccwdata.org/summary-statistics/demographics/a1-race-1999-2009.htm).

232. Glenn Beck, "Is Massive Health Care Plan Reparations?" July, 23, 2009 (Available at http://www.glennbeck.com/content/articles/article/198/28317/).

233. Alex Seitz-Wald, "The Most Widely Believed Conspiracy Theory in America Revealed in New Poll," *Alternet*, January 17, 2013.

234. Joachim Hirsch, "Globalization of Capital, Nation-States and Democracy," *Studies in Political Economy* 54 (Fall 1997), 39-58.

235. These quotes are from Paul Street, "Obama Isn't Spineless, He's Conservative: Reflections on Chutzpah, Theirs and Ours," *Zmag*, December 11, 2010.

236. Ibid.

237. Ibid.

238. Ibid.

239. Ibid.

240. Street's intention in this text is to show leftists that Obama is not progressive but rather conservative and neoliberal.

Made in the USA
Coppell, TX
17 March 2021

51850233R00075